Minnesota
"Believe It or Not"
History

by Brett Ortler

Adventure Publications, Inc.
Cambridge, MN

Acknowledgments

Many thanks to Daniel Potter for reviewing this book for accuracy. I'm also indebted to the East Central Regional Library's Cambridge Branch for their fine selection of books pertaining to Minnesota, as well as several online book depositories for their online books, including Google Books, Project Gutenberg and The Internet Archive.

Dedication

To Violet Anne.

Credits

Cover and book design by Jonathan Norberg

Photo Credits are listed on page 124.

10 9 8 7 6 5 4 3 2 1

Copyright 2015 by Brett Ortler
Published by Adventure Publications, Inc.
820 Cleveland Street South
Cambridge, MN 55008
1-800-678-7006
www.adventurepublications.net

ISBN: 978-1-59193-543-8

Introduction

Born and raised in Minnesota, I've always been fascinated with our state's past, and I'm especially drawn to just how much our state has changed over the past few centuries.

In fact, that's the primary reason I wrote this book: I wanted to provide a big-picture look at Minnesota history, one spanning from Minnesota prior to first contact with Europeans to the heyday of Minneapolis as Mill City and beyond. But I wanted things to be fun, too. That's why I've peppered the book with many funny, strange and "believe it or not" moments from our state's past.

Given how vast the subject matter is, I'm well aware that I haven't covered everything our state has to offer. On the contrary, in a book this small, I had to be selective, so I've tried to err on the side of the strange, surprising, and the plain-darn interesting. That's why I've included sidebars that delve into particularly fascinating aspects of Minnesota history—everything from a walking tour of F. Scott Fitzgerald's old St. Paul haunts to a rundown of some of Minnesota's most infamous crimes.

My goal with this book is to get you hooked on Minnesota history. To that end, I've included a listing of historical sites (see page 6) that you can visit after you're through with the book. These sites are wonderful places to learn more, and visiting them is a sure-fire way to help you put Minnesota's past into perspective.

Enjoy the book, and thanks for reading!

Table of Contents

Historic Minnesota Sites You Can Visit

You don't just have to read about Minnesota history; you can visit many of the actual locations where Minnesota history took place. The following map shows various historic sites, museums and other points of interest in Minnesota. While certainly not all-inclusive, it's a good place to begin to learn more about Minnesota's past.

METRO AREA

1. Alexander Ramsey House
2. Burial Mounds Park
3. Cathedral of St. Paul
4. Gammelgården
5. Fort Snelling
6. Foshay Tower
7. James J. Hill House
8. Landmark Center
9. Mill City Museum
10. Minnesota History Center
11. North West Company Fur Post
12. St. Anthony Falls
13. The Basilica of St. Mary
14. Sibley House Historic Site
15. State Capitol Building
16. Stone Arch Bridge
17. Wabasha Street Caves

SOUTHEAST

18. Historic Forestville
19. Pickwick Mill
20. W.W. Mayo House

SOUTHWEST

21. Alexander Harkin Store
22. Battlefield of Wood Lake
23. Birch Coulee Battlefield
24. Fort Belmont
25. Fort Ridgely
26. Jeffers Petroglyphs
27. Kensington Runestone Museum
28. La qui Parle Mission
29. Laura Ingalls Wilder Museum
30. Lower Sioux Agency
31. New Ulm
32. Pipestone National Monument
33. Sinclair Lewis Home
34. Slaughter Slough
35. Traverse des Sioux/Traverse des Sioux Treaty History Center

THE NORTHERN PART OF THE STATE

36. Bois Forte Museum
37. Charles A. Lindbergh House
38. Dorothy Molter Museum
39. *Edna G.* Tugboat
40. Forest History Center
41. Fort Ripley/Minnesota Military Museum
42. Glensheen Mansion
43. Grand Portage
44. Headwaters of Mississippi
45. Heritage Hjemkomst Museum
46. Hibbing High School
47. Hinckley Fire Museum
48. Hull-Rust-Mahoning Mine
49. Lake Superior Railroad Museum
50. Milford Mine Memorial Site
51. Mille Lacs Indian Museum
52. Minnesota Discovery Center
53. Minnesota Museum of Mining
54. Moose Lake Depot and Fires of 1918 Museum
55. Pictographs in the Boundary Waters Canoe Area Wilderness
56. Soudan Underground Mine
57. Split Rock Lighthouse
58. SS *William A. Irvin*
59. The Lost 40
60. The Northwest Angle

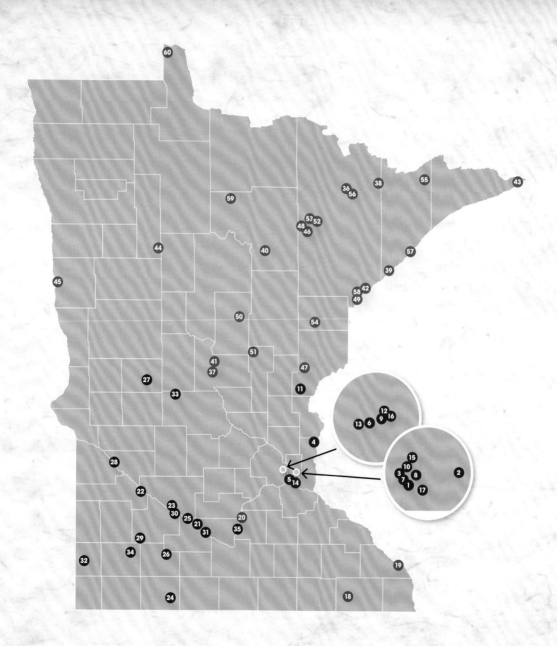

Historic Minnesota Sites You Can Visit

METRO AREA

1 Alexander Ramsey House
265 Exchange Street South
Saint Paul, MN 55102
(651) 296-8760

2 Burial Mounds Park
10 Mounds Boulevard
Saint Paul, MN 55106

3 Cathedral of St. Paul
239 Selby Avenue
Saint Paul, MN 55102
(651) 228-1766

4 Gammelgården
20880 Olinda Trail North
Scandia, MN 55073
(651) 433-5053

5 Fort Snelling
200 Tower Avenue
Saint Paul, MN 55111
(612) 726-1171

6 Foshay Tower
821 Marquette Avenue South
Minneapolis, MN 55402
(612) 215-3700

7 James J. Hill House
240 Summit Avenue
Saint Paul, MN 55102
(651) 297-2555

8 Landmark Center
75 5th Street
Saint Paul, MN 55102
(651) 292-3233

9 Mill City Museum
704 South 2nd Street
Minneapolis, MN 55401
(612) 341-7555

10 Minnesota History Center
345 West Kellogg Boulevard
Saint Paul, MN 55102
(651) 259-3000

11 North West Company Fur Post
Voyageur Lane
Pine City, MN 55063
(320) 629-6356

12 St. Anthony Falls
1 Portland Avenue
Minneapolis, MN 54401

13 The Basilica of St. Mary
88 North 17th Street
Minneapolis, MN 55403
(612) 333-1381

14 Sibley House Historic Site
1357 Sibley Memorial Highway
Mendota Heights, MN 55120
(651) 452-1596

15 State Capitol Building
75 Rev Dr Martin Luther King
Junior Boulevard
Saint Paul, MN 55155
(651) 296-2881

16 Stone Arch Bridge
1758 West River Road North
Minneapolis, MN 55411
(612) 230-6400

17 Wabasha Street Caves
215 Wabasha Street South
Saint Paul, MN 55107
(651) 224-1191

SOUTHEAST

18 Historic Forestville
21899 County Road 118
Preston, MN 55965
(507) 765-2785

19 Pickwick Mill
26421 County Road 7
Winona, MN 55987
(507) 457-3296

20 W.W. Mayo House
118 North Main Street
Le Sueur, MN 56058
(507) 665-3250

SOUTHWEST

21 Alexander Harkin Store
66250 County Road 21
New Ulm, MN 56073
(507) 354-8666

22 Battlefield of Wood Lake
www.woodlakebattlefield.com

23 Birch Coulee Battlefield
Junction of Renville County
Hwy. 2 and Hwy. 18
Morton, MN 56270

24 Fort Belmont
www.fortbelmont.org

25 Fort Ridgely
72404 County Road 30
Fairfax, MN 55332

26 Jeffers Petroglyphs
27160 510th Avenue
Comfrey, MN 56019
(507) 628-5591

27 Kensington Runestone Museum
206 Broadway Street
Alexandria, MN 56308
(320) 763-3160

28 La qui Parle Mission
http://sites.mnhs.org/
historic-sites/lac-qui-parle-
mission

29 Laura Ingalls Wilder Museum
330 8th Street
Walnut Grove, MN 56180
(800) 528-7280

30 Lower Sioux Agency
32469 Redwood County Hwy. 2
Morton, MN 56270

31 New Ulm
56073

32 Pipestone National Monument
Pipestone, MN 56164
(507) 825-5464

33 Sinclair Lewis Home
810 Sinclair Lewis Avenue
Sauk Centre, MN 56378

34 Slaughter Slough
http://murray-countymn.com/
mc/pdfs/SlaughterSlough.pdf

35 Traverse des Sioux/Traverse
des Sioux Treaty History Center
1851 North Minnesota Avenue
St. Peter, MN 56082

THE NORTHERN PART
OF THE STATE

36 Bois Forte Museum
1430 Bois Forte Road
Tower, MN 55790
(800) 992-7529

37 Charles A. Lindbergh House
1620 Lindbergh Drive South
Little Falls, MN 56345
(320) 616-5421

38 Dorothy Molter Museum
2002 East Sheridan Street
Ely, MN 55731
(218) 365-4451

39 *Edna G.* Tugboat
Agate Bay
Two Harbors, MN 55616
(218) 834-4898

40 Forest History Center
2609 County Road 76
Grand Rapids, MN 55744
(218) 327-4482

41 Fort Ripley/Minnesota Military
Museum
Camp Ripley
15000 Highway 115
Little Falls, MN 56345
(320) 616-6050

42 Glensheen Mansion
3300 London Road
Duluth, MN 55804
(218) 726-8910

43 Grand Portage
170 Mile Creek Road
Grand Portage, MN 55605
(218) 475-0123

44 Headwaters of Mississippi
Itasca State Park
36750 Main Park Drive
Park Rapids, MN 56470
(218) 699-7251

45 Heritage Hjemkomst Museum
202 1st Avenue North
Moorhead, MN 56560
(218) 299-5515

46 Hibbing High School
800 East 21st Street
Hibbing, MN 55746
(218) 208-0841

47 Hinckley Fire Museum
106 Old Hwy. 61
Hinckley, MN 55037
(320) 384-7338

48 Hull-Rust-Mahoning Mine
401 Penobscot Road
Hibbing, MN 55746
(218) 262-4166

49 Lake Superior Railroad Museum
Historic Union Depot
506 West Michigan Street
Duluth, MN 55802
(218) 727-8025

50 Milford Mine Memorial Site
http://crowwing.us/index.
aspx?NID=294

51 Mille Lacs Indian Museum
43411 Oodena Drive
Onamia, MN 56359
(320) 532-3632

52 Minnesota Discovery Center
1005 Discovery Drive
Chisholm, MN 55719
(218) 254-7959

53 Minnesota Museum of Mining
701 West Lake Street
Chisholm, MN 55719
(218) 254-5543

54 Moose Lake Depot and Fires of
1918 Museum
900 Folz Boulevard
Moose Lake, MN 55767
(218) 485-4234

55 Pictographs in the Boundary
Waters Canoe Area Wilderness
www.fs.usda.gov/detail/
superior/

56 Soudan Underground Mine
Soudan Underground Mine
State Park
1302 McKinley Park Road
Soudan, MN 55782
(218) 753-2245

57 Split Rock Lighthouse
Split Rock Lighthouse State Park
3713 Split Rock Lighthouse Rd.
Two Harbors, MN 55616
(218) 226-6372

58 SS *William A. Irvin*
50 Harbor Drive
Duluth, MN 55802
(218) 722-7876

59 The Lost 40
www.fs.usda.gov/recarea/
chippewa/recreation/re-
carea/?recid=26672&actid=70

60 The Northwest Angle
www.dnr.state.mn.us/state_
forests/sft00036/index.html

Note: Because some sites
are open seasonally, be
sure to call ahead or check
online before visiting!

From Prehistory to Settlement (prehistory – 1850s)

Minnesota's history didn't start with the arrival of French explorers in the seventeenth century. On the contrary, Minnesota has been inhabited by American Indians for thousands of years. This is an overview of Minnesota's earliest history and covers everything from a discussion of when (and how) people may first have arrived in Minnesota to the perennially popular debate about supposed Viking relics in Minnesota.

View of burial mounds in St. Paul

HOW—AND WHEN—DID PEOPLE FIRST ARRIVE IN NORTH AMERICA?

When did people first arrive in North America? This simple question is one of the most hotly debated questions in archaeology. You're probably familiar with the traditional theory, which states that people first entered North America via the Bering Land Bridge. Today, the Bering Sea is a vast, cold place perhaps best known because of shows like *The Deadliest Catch*. But approximately 20,000 years ago, during the most recent glacial period, sea

Alaska and the Bering Strait

levels were much lower (as the glacial ice essentially stockpiled much of the water), and what is now the bottom of the Bering Sea was exposed, creating a "bridge" to North America.[1] Over the span of thousands of years, scientists suggest, people made their way across this bridge and into North America,

pre-history — 1650s

dispersing across the continent by about 12,000 years ago. Often referred to as the Clovis People, these settlers get their name from an archaeological site found near Clovis, New Mexico, and they are known for the distinctive characteristics of their stone tools. For decades, the Clovis People were deemed the first inhabitants of North America.

Believe It or Not

According to DNA studies and forensic anthropology, modern humans have existed for only 160,000 years.[2] Compared to other species, that's not much. Some turtle species have existed for something like 220 million years.[3]

THE COASTAL THEORY

Thanks to a number of important archaeological discoveries, the Bering Sea theory has recently come under scrutiny.[4] A new hypothesis posits that humans made their way from Asia and the South Pacific via boats. This idea has recently been bolstered by a number of discoveries, including a very old archaeological site in Chile that is older than what the "bridge" theory predicts (14,000 years old!).[5] Recent DNA studies have confirmed this rough timeline.[6] Many experts now hypothesize that people probably made their way to North America by land *and* by sea.

Believe It or Not

A number of scientists have argued that boats may have been in use as much as 40,000 years ago, and maybe even further back.[7] One group of scientists has argued that Neanderthals, not humans, were the first seafarers and that they may have taken to the seas tens of thousands of years before we did.[8]

GRANDPA CAVEMAN

DNA studies of early humans have revealed something else; while Neanderthals are commonly depicted as cavemen, don't knock them: if you're of European or Asian descent, you're part Neanderthal. According to a

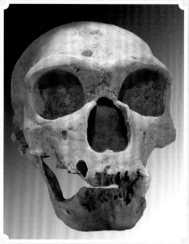
A Neanderthal skull

groundbreaking genetic study, about 2.5 percent of the DNA of folks of European or Asian descent originated with Neanderthals.[9] The current theory is that as groups of humans began migrating out of Africa, one population headed toward Europe, where they encountered Neanderthals and interbred with them on a small scale.

THE FIRST MINNESOTANS: GUESSES AT THE EARLIEST PEOPLE IN MINNESOTA

So let's get back to Minnesota's history. As archaeologist Guy Gibbon notes in his book, *Archaeology of Minnesota*, historical accounts of Minnesota start in the seventeenth century, but according to archaeological evidence, Minnesota has been peopled for at least 13,000 years.[10] (For a frame of reference, the famous pyramids at Giza are less than five thousand years old.) This means that the vast majority of Minnesota's human habitation is often ignored.

A LONG HISTORY

Generally speaking, archaeologists classify Minnesota's American Indian artifacts and sites by time period. In this system, there are three primary time periods. The oldest period is the Paleoindian, which is followed by the Archaic, and then the Woodland period, which is split into two parts: the "initial" and "terminal" period. To give you an idea of the time frame, this is a rough timeline of the American Indian sites found near the Rainy River:[11]

Paleoindian period, (10,900–7,500 BC)[12]
Archaic period (7,500–500 BC)
Woodland period (500 BC–1,650 AD)
    —Initial Woodland (500 BC–1,000 AD)
    —Terminal Woodland (1000–1,650 AD)

pre-history
1650s

Believe It or Not

Given that the Paleoindians who inhabited Minnesota were constantly on the move and had comparatively small populations, there are very few Paleoindian artifacts known from Minnesota. In fact, there are only 19 on record, 17 of which are weapon points.[13] This doesn't mean the Paleoindians were warlike; they were hunters, and their weapon points were made of very durable materials that could persist over millennia. Unfortunately, none of the more-fragile artifacts that they undoubtedly carried (clothing, etc.) seem to have survived.

SOME BIG CHANGES

The cultural, technological and societal differences between the Paleoindian period and the poorly named "terminal" Woodland period are profound.

Blackduck-style pottery discovered in a mound near Rainy River

Paleoindian culture consisted of small bands of hunter-gatherers who were constantly on the move as they hunted large animals. By the Woodland period, American Indian cultures supported a much larger population, had very different social structures, made pottery, buried their dead, relied on an entirely different food base (often one that incorporated horticulture) and resided in semi-temporary encampments.[14] Despite the differences between the archaeological periods, one thing is clear: American Indian cultures have adapted, survived and thrived in Minnesota over the course of thousands of years despite huge climactic, environmental and social changes. Too often in American culture, our image of American Indian culture is monolithic and static, but archaeology shows that it is anything but.

Believe It or Not

Many American Indian cultures buried their dead in burial mounds, and the mounds vary as much as the various cultures who created them. Some mounds are positively massive—hundreds of feet long and wide and dozens of feet high, so large that it's easy to mistake them for natural landforms. Others are hardly noticeable. Minnesota is home to over 12,000 mounds alone; Indian Mounds Park in St. Paul is named for the mounds found there, though many have since been destroyed because of shoddy archaeology and outright tomb raiding.[15, 16]

MINNESOTA'S AMERICAN INDIANS TELL A VERY DIFFERENT STORY

American Indians are often skeptical of archaeology and its claims. In many respects, they have good reason. Archaeology—like all science—is not immune to prejudice, and many injustices were wrought in its name. Burial mounds were looted or destroyed altogether, and bodies were put on display. Perhaps even more insulting, Europeans, including some archaeologists, argued that the massive burial mounds were "too advanced" to have been created by American Indians. (This same attitude can be seen in those who insist that the Pyramids at Giza and other megalithic monuments must have been created by "ancient astronomers" because the indigenous inhabitants were "too primitive" to complete them.)

THE SAME STATE, BUT A DIFFERENT PLACE

Perhaps the best way to understand Minnesota's history is to understand what Minnesota looked like on the day before Europeans first entered Minnesota. The landscape was profoundly different. The virgin forests of the northland were unlogged and the area's white pines were gargantuan: 100-foot-tall trees were common, and the tallest specimens were perhaps over 100 feet taller (and maybe even larger).[17, 18] Throughout the state, the swamp-loving tamarack was the most populous tree species, which makes sense given that none of Minnesota's many wetlands had been drained yet.[19] Since settlement, over half of Minnesota's wetlands have been drained.[20] Perhaps the most profound change, however, came on the prairie. Often depicted as a sea of grass, the prairie stretched across 18 million acres of Minnesota, and it teemed with wildlife, including the now-vanished bison.[21]

More importantly, North America and South America were brimming with people. While expert estimates range widely, it's quite clear that there were millions of American Indians in North America when Europeans arrived, and tens of millions spread throughout North and South America.[22]

pre-
history
1650s

Believe It or Not

In popular culture, American Indian cultures are often depicted as living in small-scale settlements, but that wasn't always the case. Some of the cities that Europeans encountered were positively massive. Located in present-day Mexico City, the Aztec capital of Tenochtitlan (pronounced *tay-notch-teet-lon*) was built on an island in the center of a marshy lake. (Over centuries, the lake was essentially reclaimed and the island expanded.)[23] When Europeans arrived, they encountered a city of floating gardens and canals, and the city boasted perhaps 100,000 to 200,000 people. At the time, it was one of the largest cities in the world, maybe even the largest.

THE DAKOTA NATION: THE SEVEN COUNCIL FIRES

At the time of first contact, there were two primary groups of American Indians in what would become Minnesota: The Dakota and The Ojibwe.

The Dakota Nation (sometimes referred to by the term Sioux) consists of seven bands that are collectively referred to as the Seven Council Fires.[24] Taken together, their territory spanned across much of the Upper Midwest, including much of Minnesota. At the time of first contact, the Santee, the Mdewakanton, Wahpekute, Wahpeton and Sisseton all lived in the eastern portion of the Dakota Nation's territory, residing primarily in Minnesota and northern Iowa.[25] Taken together, these groups are often labeled the Eastern Dakota.

Located in the middle of the Dakota Nation's historic range, the Yankton and the Yanktonai lived in the eastern portions of North and South Dakota prior to contact with Europeans.[26] These two groups are sometimes called the "Nakota."

The Teton, also known as the Lakota, bordered the Yankton and Yanktonai to the west, and lived in western North Dakota, extending into northern Nebraska.

DIFFERENT PLACE, DIFFERENT LIFESTYLE

Even prior to contact, there were important differences between the cultures of the various council fires of the Dakota Nation. In the east, the Santee culture was a woodland culture based on harvesting wild rice, maple syruping, fishing and hunting.[27] By contrast, on the plains, where prairie dominated, bison played an incredibly important part in the life of the Lakota.

THE OJIBWE: A GROUP ON THE MOVE

The Ojibwe (also known as the Chippewa or the Anishinabe) began to live in Minnesota sometime in the seventeenth century; according to Ojibwe tradition, their journey to the Minnesota region had seven stops, each of which was presaged by a prophet.[28] They would know their "chosen ground" when they found the "rice that floats on water," which we know as wild rice.[29] The migration route was a winding one, beginning on the eastern seaboard near Maine and eventually leading to northeastern Minnesota and northwestern Wisconsin.

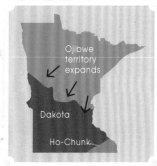

American Indian territories from 1650 to 1805

TROUBLE TO THE EAST

The Ojibwe had another reason to migrate—they spent much of the 1600s fighting the ascendant Iroquois Nation, which had been armed by Europeans and was attempting to control the lucrative fur market, the same motivation that would eventually lead the voyageurs to visit Minnesota. This conflict—known as the Beaver War—had an important impact on Minnesota, as it compelled the Ojibwe to move westward, though they more than held their own against the Iroquois.[30]

pre-
history
1650s

Dakota and Ojibwe Indian-Inspired Places and Names

Prior to European settlement, all place names in Minnesota stemmed from Dakota or Ojibwe. It's therefore not surprising that many of the same terms are still in use today. Here are just a few examples.

DAKOTA

Minnesota first referred to the Minnesota River and its "cloud-tinted waters"

Anoka is a combination of two words referring to a neutral area between the Dakota and the Ojibwe[i]

Blue Earth is a translation of a Dakota description of the area's blue soil, which gets it color thanks to a bluish clay

Chanhassen is named for the Dakota word for the sugar maple tree[ii]

Chaska is a name often given to the firstborn son in a Dakota family

Isanti means "knife" and is a reference to Knife Lake in Mora; the "Santee" are a major division of the Dakota

Kandiyohi means "abounding in buffalo fish" in Dakota[iii]

Mahtomedi means "the gray bear lake" in Dakota

Mille Lacs now bears a French name meaning "Thousand Lakes," but the Dakota originally referred to the lake as *Mde Wakan*, which translates as "Spirit Lake," and the area held (and holds) a deep spiritual importance to the Dakota

Minnehaha is a somewhat poetic European mistranslation of the Dakota phrase, "curling water" or "waterfalls;" because Minnehaha already means "waterfall," Minnehaha Falls literally means "Waterfalls Falls"

Minneiska means "water white" in Dakota[iv]

Minneopa means "water falling twice," a reference to the waterfalls of Minneopa Creek[v]

Minnetonka is a combination of the Dakota words for "big" and "water"[vi]

Minnewashta means "good water"

The Rum River was known as the "Spirit River" by the Dakota; this name was mistranslated by later settlers as the "Rum River"

Shakopee means "six" and refers to a Dakota Chief named Sakpe[VII]

Sleepy Eye is named in honor of a Dakota chief, Sleepy Eye, who had drooping eyelids

Waconia means "spring" or "fountain" in Dakota[VIII]

Wahpeton is the name for a large, forest-dwelling division of the Dakota[IX]

White Bear Lake references a visit to the area by a polar bear or a grizzly[X]

Winona is a name often given to the firstborn daughter in a Dakota family

Yellow Medicine refers to the name of a plant once used by the Dakota for medicinal purposes[XI]

OJIBWE

Chisago is a conversion of an Ojibwe phrase meaning "lovely lake"

Crow Wing is something of a disputed name that apparently stems from the Ojibwe name for the Crow Wing River[I]

Cut Foot Sioux Lake is named for a site where a Dakota Indian died during a battle

Kabetogama means "runs parallel with another lake"[II]

Kanabec is the Ojibwe name for "snake" and stems from the nearby Snake River

Koochiching is a name of disputed origin and may mean "at the place of the inlets" in Ojibwe

Mahnomen is the Ojibwe word for wild rice

Otter Tail is a translation of the Ojibwe phrase describing a sandbar with an otter tail-like shape in Otter Tail Lake[III]

Pokegama is a name given to a lake with many branches[IV]

Superior was first known as *Gichigami*, or the great sea

Thief River Falls is named for the Thief River, which originates from an Ojibwe phrase

Wadena means "little round hill" in Ojibwe and refers to area bluffs[V]

Winnibigoshish means "dirty water"

pre-
history
1650s

EUROPEANS ARRIVE IN NORTH AMERICA: CHRISTOPHER COLUMBUS AND SOME BAD MATH

Columbus arriving in the New World

Any discussion of the European exploration of Minnesota (and North America, generally) would be incomplete without a discussion of Christopher Columbus. Often heralded for discovering the New World, Columbus's primary goal wasn't that different from the later explorers probing for the Northwest Passage: he wanted to find a simpler trade route to India. His discovery of North America was essentially an accident, and one that only occurred because Columbus woefully miscalculated the circumference of the world (he was off by over twelve thousand miles).[32] Columbus's landing in America was essentially the result of a series of math errors.

THE COLUMBIAN EXCHANGE: THE GOOD AND THE (REALLY) BAD

While it may sound like parlance for a South American drug deal, the Columbian Exchange refers to the lifeforms and organisms that were transferred when the Old World and the New World first made contact. Given how long ago the exchange occurred, and how important some of species are now to various cultures, it can be easy to forget that just a few hundred years ago, many plants, animals and diseases that we take for granted were unknown in some parts of the world. For example, there were no potatoes in Ireland or tomatoes in Italy. Prior to settlement of the New World, tobacco was unknown in Europe. In the New World, coffee and sugar were introduced, as were livestock, such as horses. Unfortunately, diseases were also inadvertently traded.[33] When Columbus and other explorers arrived, they brought smallpox, measles, typhus and cholera with them. As these diseases were unheard of in the New World, the aboriginal populations had no immunity to them.[34] This led to massive population losses in the native populations. As the frontier expanded westward, successive populations were affected, including ones in Minnesota, killing millions.

WERE VIKINGS THE FIRST EUROPEANS IN MINNESOTA?

Life in the Viking Age (stamp from the Faroe Islands)

Of course, a discussion of the first Europeans in Minnesota would be incomplete without discussing Alexandria's claim to fame: the Kensington Runestone, a large slab of stone inscribed with runes found on a rural farm. Alleged to date back to 1362, the Runestone is often put forth as proof that the Vikings were the first Europeans to visit Minnesota. While the Vikings certainly did visit North America prior to Columbus—about 492 years before!—they settled in what is now Nova Scotia at a settlement often referred to as Vinland. According to archaeologists and experts in Scandinavian languages, the Runestone is a hoax, and the Vikings never made their way into Minnesota.[31] Nonetheless, as the staff at the Runestone Museum in Minnesota will tell you, not everyone agrees with that opinion.

RADISSON AND GROSEILLIERS

Europeans first visited North America in 1492, but they wouldn't visit Minnesota until nearly 200 years later. The first Europeans to visit Minnesota were a pair of French explorers and businessmen: Pierre-Esprit Radisson and Médard Chouart, Sieur des Groseilliers. Leaving from Quebec, they first arrived in Minnesota sometime in the late 1650s (most sources say 1659). Over the course of the next decade, they traveled throughout much of the state, staying at present-day Duluth, near Mille Lacs Lake, and in the vicinity of the Mississippi River.

1650s
1670s

A beaver-skin top hat

BUSINESS INTERESTS

Radisson and Groseilliers weren't exploring for exploration's sake; they were business-men. Specifically, they were interested in acquiring beaver pelts. While the initial exploration of North America (and Minnesota) was dedicated to finding the fabled Northwest Passage, a trade route that would connect the Atlantic to the Pacific, later ventures focused on the resources found throughout North America. Much of the fur trade centered on beavers, as beaver fur was in high demand for use in beaver hats.[35] The demand was so great that beavers practically went extinct in Europe.[36]

Believe It or Not

In a real respect, much of the initial settlement of North America was driven by a fashion craze.

THE HUDSON BAY COMPANY

Radisson and Groseilliers returned to Quebec with a veritable armada of canoes, all full of furs, but encountered resistance from the French authorities, who refused to allow them a trade permit, confiscated their furs and fined them.[37] After continued trouble with the French, Radisson and Groseilliers eventually found British benefactors who financed their fur-gathering venture, which was successful. In 1670, a Royal Charter was issued, and the famous Hudson Bay Company was formed. It dominated the fur trade in much of North America for two centuries. At its peak, it boasted the power and territory of a full-fledged country.

Believe It or Not

The Hudson Bay Company is still in operation. Today, they primarily operate in real estate and retail. They own and run Saks Fifth Avenue, among other stores.

THE FIRST RECORDED MISSING PERSONS CASE IN THE REGION

Other Frenchmen soon visited the region, and one of them would never return home. René Ménard was the first missionary to visit the region, and his story doesn't end happily.[38, 39, 40] Judging by the letter that he wrote before he left, Ménard was well aware of the dangers. He wrote to a fellow priest, "In three or four months you may remember me at the memento for the dead . . ."[41]

While attempting to bring food to a group of American Indians, he disappeared somewhere in Wisconsin, and his fate has been a mystery since 1661.

THE FIRST MAP OF LAKE SUPERIOR

Soon after Ménard's disappearance, a new priest was sent to replace him. Father Claude Allouez's visit is perhaps most notable for the map of Lake Superior that he and Father Marquette produced. Published in 1670, it has some clear errors, but it is still the first recorded map of the big lake.

1670s
1680s

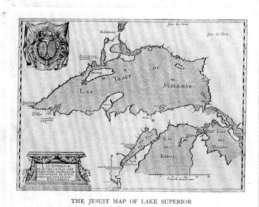

THE JESUIT MAP OF LAKE SUPERIOR
(From the Relation of 1670–1671)

The Jesuit Map of Lake Superior

MOST OF MINNESOTA BECOMES NEW FRANCE (AT LEAST TECHNICALLY)

Missionaries weren't the only Frenchmen to visit. After reports of the many natural resources became known, explorers were sent with territorial ambitions. The historical record is a bit messy, as there are several French claims of "ownership" of parts of Minnesota, but all in all the scene wasn't that different from the "I

1670s
1750s

claim this land in the name of Spain" scene depicted in the famous *Looney Tunes* cartoons.[42, 43] Essentially, a representative of the government arrived, read a document declaring ownership of the land and "welcomed" the indigenous population as subjects of the king. (They were also directed to convert to Catholicism.) Never mind the fact that the document read to the indigenous population was read in only one language and the areas claimed were so vast that they were peopled by entirely different American Indian Nations. For example, René-Robert Cavelier, Sieur de La Salle, claimed the *entire* Mississippi Basin in the name of France. By 1682, most of Minnesota was at least technically French territory.

Believe It or Not

At the 1671 ceremony where France claimed possession of the Lake Superior region, the French gathered a number of American Indian nations and acquired their "consent," welcoming them to the French Empire. The Dakota Nation, who inhabited the vast majority of Minnesota, never even got an invite.[44] What's worse, the American Indian groups at such ceremonies had no conception that the French were actually claiming to own the land; they likely thought it was some sort of trade ritual.[45]

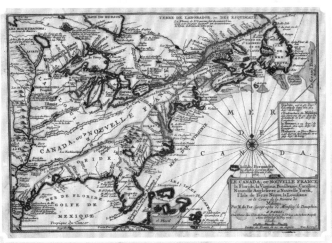

A map of New France circa 1703

NOT MUCH OF AN OFFICIAL FRENCH PRESENCE

Even though the French claimed that Minnesota was French territory, there was no real military presence in Minnesota until much later. The tale of Daniel Greysolon, Sieur Du Lhut, a military man who claimed the Mille Lacs area for France in 1679, is typical.[46] He almost literally planted a flag, then left. (He actually adhered a French Royal emblem to a tree.)[47] The first French outpost was built in the late 1690s, but a true French fort—Fort Beauharnois—wasn't built until 1727.[48, 49]

Believe It or Not

As you probably realize, Duluth, Minnesota, gets its name from Daniel Greysolon, Sieur Du Lhut, but there are many variations on the spelling of his name; thankfully, some of the odder variants, including Du Lude and Dulhut, were not adopted as his namesake.

BREAKING THE LAW

Instead of soldiers, French priests and traders dominated the land that would become Minnesota. Many of the traders in early Minnesota were known as *coureurs de bois*—which literally means "woods runner"—and they traded in pelts without a license from the French provincial government.[50] Legally speaking, this made them outlaws of a sort, but Minnesota's remoteness essentially made it a region where the French government in Quebec had little to no actual power.

RISE OF THE VOYAGEURS

Eventually, France began to assert some control over the region. A number of forts were established in or near Minnesota in the early eighteenth century, and soon the voyageurs became the primary face of the fur trade in Minnesota. While the *coureurs de bois* were unlicensed, the voyageurs (French for "travelers") were essentially hired help and worked on behalf of a licensed trader.[51] Voyageurs were instantly recognizable due to their attire— loose-fitting clothes, colorful sashes

Voyageurs in Minnesota

**1670s
1750s**

and sturdy moccasins—and even due to their size.[52] Voyageurs were often very stocky and rather short, as this body frame was most conducive to work in a fully packed canoe. They needed all the muscle they could get, too; the work they did was intense. Traveling primarily by canoe, they traveled down treacherous rivers, ran dangerous rapids, and traveled in small boats on the Great Lakes. When they couldn't travel on the water, they were responsible for carrying their gear overland, no simple feat given the weight (180 pounds!) of the furs they were expected to carry.

Believe It or Not

While the average voyageur was expected to carry two bundles of furs, some carried more. According to one account, a six-foot-five freed slave named La Bonga became a voyageur after carrying a record nine bundles of fur for a half mile.[53] If true, that means he carried 630 pounds of furs.

JESUIT INFLUENCE

Operating a series of missions throughout the Great Lakes region, Jesuit priests were the first Europeans to visit many of the Minnesota landmarks we know today. Among the most famous Jesuits to visit Minnesota, Father Hennepin was the first European to visit St. Anthony Falls, which he named. After his travels in what was then known as Louisiana—much of Minnesota was later part of the Louisiana Purchase—Hennepin returned to France and published a rather sensational account of his trip, *A Description of Louisiana*. In it, he claimed that the falls were 50 to 60 feet high, but later explorers estimated they were about a third of that.[54, 55]

St. Anthony Falls before development

Believe It or Not

Father Hennepin's book was the first one written about Minnesota.

TROUBLE IN NEW FRANCE

By the middle of the eighteenth century, New France was in serious trouble. Immersed in the Seven Years' War, a much wider conflict involving much of Europe, France was pressured by the British Colonies to the east, which were militarily superior. After an initial series of defeats, the British soundly defeated the French in North America. (The North American portion of the Seven Years' War is known as the French and Indian War in the U.S.)

MINNESOTA AS HOT POTATO

1760s 1770s

The Seven Years' War finally ended with the signing of the Treaty of Paris in 1763. As a condition of the treaty, the French ceded all land east of the Mississippi to the British, including roughly half of Minnesota. The land to the west of the Mississippi went to the Spanish, so with the stroke of a pen, half of Minnesota's citizens became inhabitants of either the Spanish or British empires. Spain's claim to part of Minnesota's territory lasted until 1803, but no Spaniards actually officially visited Minnesota, and no one even bothered to tell the actual American Indian inhabitants of the area.[56] After the American Revolution, the British territory east of the Mississippi was ceded to the United States. The Minnesota land to the east of the Mississippi became part of the Northwest Territory. In 1803, President Thomas Jefferson purchased the land west of the Mississippi from France in the famed Louisiana Purchase. (France had only recently regained the territory from its ally Spain.) The (already inhabited!) land went for an absolute pittance; it was bought for about five cents an acre.[57]

1760s
1770s

Believe It or Not

The man who sold the land of the Louisiana Purchase to the U.S.? None other than Napoleon Bonaparte.

JONATHAN CARVER, OWNER OF THE MINNESOTA CAPITOL BUILDING?

After the end of the Seven Years' War, part of the land that would become Minnesota came under British control, but practically speaking, not a lot

Jonathan Carver

changed. There were no official expeditions, but one English-speaking explorer—Jonathan Carver—did visit the region in search of the fabled Northwest Passage. While he didn't break much ground by way of geography, he did spend the winter with the Dakota and produce an English-language book describing his travels— *Travels Through the Interior Parts of North America.* Carver also left a strange imprint on popular culture: his heirs later claimed that Carver was granted a huge swath of land by his Dakota hosts.[58, 59] In all, the claim spanned from east of the Mississippi at St. Anthony Falls and across much of Wisconsin. The matter was eventually brought to Congress—and since no original deed was found—it was dismissed.[60] If the Carver family had succeeded in acquiring the land allegedly signed to Carver, they would now own the Capitol Building and much of St. Paul, not to mention a huge chunk of Wisconsin.

Believe It or Not

Bizarrely, Carver's story has given rise to a ghost story in which the ghost of Jonathan Carver is alleged to haunt Summerwind, a now-ruined mansion within the territory of Carver's alleged grant.[61] According to the story, Carver's long-lost deed was said to have been hidden in Summerwind's foundation, and Carver's ghost would plague the house until the deed was found. Despite many searches for the deed, it was never found. Then again, the source of this story isn't all that credible; he reportedly got his information from the long-dead Jonathan Carver himself, communicating via a ouija board, dreams and trances.[62]

A DIFFERENT FUR TRADE: THE NORTH WEST COMPANY

French influence in the region was on the wane, in part because of a change in tactics in the fur trade. Whereas the French were operating primarily on rivers and the Great Lakes, other traders—often of Scottish descent—headed deep inland to acquire more furs. Later, these groups consolidated, creating the North West Company.[63] It would become the arch-rival of the Hudson Bay Company and dominate the fur trade in Minnesota. Its headquarters were originally based at Grand Portage, and over the next few decades, the North West Company would establish posts across much of Minnesota.[64]

THE REDCOATS ARE COMING . . . TO GRAND PORTAGE

1770s
1805

During the Revolutionary War, Minnesota was obviously not a hotspot for conflict; nonetheless, on one occasion, it was actually visited by British troops during the war. Because of its importance as a regional trade hub, traders encouraged the British government to send a handful of troops to Grand Portage to ensure that trading went on uneventfully.[65] A group of thirteen soldiers (one officer and 12 regulars) arrived on an armed sloop. They stayed for two months, the only military presence in Minnesota on either side during the Revolutionary War.

A REVOLUTIONARY WAR VETERAN BURIED IN MINNESOTA

Minnesota has another Revolutionary War connection: Stephen Taylor, a veteran of the Continental Army, is buried in Minnesota, outside Winona. [66] While much is in debate about his life—including his age and the specific battles he fought in—records indicate that he did serve in George Washington's Continental Army for three years. According to Taylor's account, he even met Washington himself. Taylor moved to Minnesota (then the extreme frontier) after the war. Taylor lived quite some time, dying in 1857.

THE JAY TREATY

Even though the U.S. was victorious against the British in the Revolutionary War, the British continued to obstruct the new federal government wherever possible. Minnesota (and the rest of the frontier) was the perfect place to do that. Just as the French Empire held little power over the land that would become Minnesota, the fledgling American government had almost no military power in the region. The British took advantage of this and refused to leave the military and commercial posts they had established (even though they'd agreed to do so at the end of the Revolutionary War.)[67] Only after the signing of the Jay Treaty in 1794 did the American government begin to exert more influence in the region. Even still, trade was largely dominated by Europeans.[68]

American Indian territories in 1805

ZEBULON PIKE AND THE FIRST SEARCH FOR THE HEADWATERS

The U.S. government eventually began to take a more serious interest in the frontier in the early nineteenth century. At around the same time Lewis and Clark were ordered to reach the Pacific, Army Lieutenant Zebulon Pike was dispatched to explore the Mississippi River in order to find a suitable site for a future military base and to ascertain what resources were in the region. While Pike didn't succeed in discovering the Headwaters of the Mississippi—he named Cass Lake as their source—in 1805 he did meet with local Dakota leaders. Two of them signed a treaty—often described as the first in Minnesota history—that ceded 100,000 acres of land at the junction of the Mississippi and Minnesota Rivers.[69] Pike estimated that the land was worth a fortune, $200,000, but the U.S. government only offered $2,000 much later, and paid it decades late.[70, 71] Worse yet, the treaty was written in English and translated by government-paid interpreters, and it wasn't actually authorized by the Senate. Given that the area being sold was and is revered by the Dakota as one of their holiest places—it features directly into one of the Dakota's creation stories—it's unlikely that the two Dakota who signed the treaty would have agreed had they known what was at stake.[72] To put it in Judeo-Christian terms, it was the equivalent of selling paradise for a pittance.

Believe It or Not

Pike's legacy is a strange one, especially since it is marred by an alleged connection to then-Vice President Aaron Burr. Remember him? In addition to being famous for killing Alexander Hamilton in a duel, Burr was also suspected of plotting to have a large portion of the then-American West secede from the U.S. (It's not exactly clear which areas figured into Burr's plan, exactly, as the details are quite fuzzy.)[73]

Long story short: Burr was collaborating with General James Wilkinson, the man who ordered Pike to travel up the Mississippi and without the approval of President Jefferson. Wilkinson was the main figure helping Burr plan his murky insurrection (they even had their own secret code!). It's not clear whether Pike was a willing participant of his commanding officer's scheme or not, but his reputation has been somewhat sullied by the close association with Wilkinson.

Zebulon Pike

FORT SNELLING AND THE BEGINNINGS OF THE TWIN CITIES

The land that Pike obtained would play an incredibly important role in the future development of Minnesota, as it would become the site of Fort Snelling. Located at the confluence of the Mississippi and the Minnesota Rivers, the site was a natural transportation and trade hub, and a sturdy limestone fort was built upon the bluffs there in 1825.[74] The fort would figure into some of the most important scenes in early Minnesota history—and some of the darkest.

1805
—
1830s

Fort Snelling

1805–1830s

Believe It or Not

Once Fort Snelling was established, weather observations at the site began to be recorded consistently; they provide some of the oldest consistent weather readings in U.S. history. Weather records have been kept there nearly continuously since 1819, when the fort was just under construction.[75]

THE TREATY ERA BEGINS

The ongoing hostilities between the Ojibwe and the Dakota in the eighteenth century continued into the beginning of the nineteenth century. By this time, the Ojibwe primarily occupied the northern two-thirds of the state and the Dakota occupied the southern third of the state. After the War of 1812, which had little effect on Minnesota, the U.S. government began to take an active interest in its western territories. The Prairie du Chien treaty of 1825, backed up by the presence of U.S. Army regulars at Fort Snelling, established official (but often disregarded) borders between the Dakota and the Ojibwe, and it also served another purpose—by defining clear boundaries, it helped make the purchase of American Indian lands easier in the future.[76, 77]

The Search for the Headwaters, Renewed

While Zebulon Pike and a subsequent expedition had declared (incorrectly) that Cass Lake was the source of the Mississippi, Henry Schoolcraft didn't believe it. A geologist and the Indian Agent for the Michigan region, he set out in 1832 to identify the river's true source. From his close contacts with the Ojibwe in the region, Schoolcraft was well aware that Elk Lake was the true source of the great river. The voyage, aided by Schoolcraft's Ojibwe guide Ozawindib, confirmed what the Ojibwe already knew, and the Headwaters region officially found its claim to fame. Schoolcraft's findings were confirmed four years later when a Frenchman with a famous surname, Jean Nicollet, extensively mapped the Headwaters region.

The famous Headwaters signpost

Believe It or Not

Lake Itasca is a made-up name. Before Schoolcraft dubbed it Lake Itasca, it was originally known as Lac La Biche (meaning Elk Lake, a translation of the Ojibwe name for the Lake: Omashkooz, which referred to the antler-like outline of the lake).[78] Schoolcraft, perhaps wanting to glamorize the discovery of the lake (and cement his place in history) asked one of his traveling companions how to say "true head" in Latin. Schoolcraft arbitrarily created the name Itasca from the middle of the phrase: "*veritas caput.*" He even made up an Indian "legend" to go along with it. (As it turns out, the companion got the translation wrong: *veritas caput* actually means "truth head.")

1830s **1840s**

GLAZIER'S "DISCOVERIES"

Given the remoteness of Lake Itasca and the Headwaters, Schoolcraft's discovery wasn't immediately universally accepted. On the contrary, other explorers also wanted to make their own discoveries and set out to "discover" the Headwaters. Perhaps the most colorful was Captain Willard Glazier, who set out in 1881 to "discover" the true source of the Mississippi. After visiting the region, he claimed that a nearby lake was the Mississippi's true source; he quickly renamed the lake (which was also named Elk Lake) "Lake Glazier" in honor of himself.[79] In his account of the trip—*Down the Great River*—he even had the gall to plagiarize whole sections from Henry Schoolcraft's account. He financed a second trip to bolster his claims, but to little avail.

THE TREATIES OF 1837

Whereas Minnesota had largely been a backwater at the beginning of the 1800s, it soon began to take on more importance. This was the heyday of Manifest Destiny, and Minnesota was considered the heart of the "northwestern" frontier, and a land ripe with resources (especially timber) and an eventual destination for settlement. After the Prairie du Chien treaty of 1825, the U.S. concluded two small treaties in the early 1830s before concluding two major treaties, one with the Ojibwe, which ceded 12 million acres (including Lake Mille Lacs), and another with the Dakota, which netted the U.S. much of the Dakota's land east of the Mississippi. The Ojibwe received a pittance for their land—all told, the

**1830s
1840s**

U.S. paid about $194,000, and only a small amount went to the Ojibwe, with much going to settle debts with traders.[80,81] The Dakota fared just as poorly; originally summoned to Washington under the guise of establishing the southern boundary of their territory, they were instead cajoled into giving up their land east of the Mississippi.[82]

Believe It or Not

Once Fort Snelling was established, adventurous settlers began to flock to the area, which was at the very edge of the frontier. This attracted a varied cast of characters, including Pierre "Pig's Eye" Parrant, who set up a saloon in a cave in St. Paul in 1838.[83] His land claim was the first in St. Paul, and the early town was known as "Pig's Eye Landing" until 1841 when Lucien Galtier, a Roman Catholic missionary, built a chapel dedicated to St. Paul, giving the city its current name.

THE INDIAN REMOVAL ACT

The notion of Manifest Destiny had a grim counterpart: the Indian Removal Act, which was signed by President Andrew Jackson and authorized Congress to remove American Indian nations, often forcibly, and settle them on land west of the Mississippi. While Indian Removal is often associated with tribes in the south and southwestern portions of the country, the same motivations were behind the dealings with the Ojibwe and Dakota in Minnesota.

MINNESOTA BECOMES A TERRITORY

After being part of several U.S. territories, Minnesota became its own territory in 1849. This might seem surprising, given that the Dakota and the Ojibwe had actually ceded only a portion of what would become Minnesota at that point; nonetheless, in the mind of those in power, it was already a forgone conclusion that other land would follow. Sure enough, in 1851, a huge part of Minnesota was ceded to the U.S. by the Dakota.

President Andrew Jackson

**1840s
1850s**

Believe It or Not

For a time, the boundaries of what would become Minnesota were in considerable flux; St. Anthony Falls were especially coveted and they nearly became part of Wisconsin, and horror of horrors, even part of Iowa.[84] Thankfully for Minnesota, these amendments were voted down.

Despite popular images like this, most settlers arrived by steamboat.

Believe It or Not

Prior to 1805, no treaties had been enacted between the U.S. government and American Indian nations in Minnesota. By the 1860s, over a dozen treaties had been enacted, and nearly all American Indian lands in Minnesota—Dakota and Ojibwe alike—had been purchased by the United States Government.

Believe It or Not

In some cases, the reservations that were set aside for American Indian tribes were never actually created, and in others, the tribe was moved to a reservation, only to be moved again when that land was in demand. The Ho-Chunk (also known as the Winnebago) are a notable example, having been forced to move many times.[85]

SETTLERS ARRIVE AND FORTS GO UP

Once Minnesota became a territory, settlers began to flood in, and the government quickly built forts to project military power and to protect the territory's new inhabitants.[86] In a little over a decade, three primitive forts—Fort Ripley, Fort Ridgely and Fort Abercrombie (now located in North Dakota) all went up. Fort Ridgely in particular would play an incredibly important role in Minnesota's history, as it would figure heavily into the U.S.-Dakota War.

Believe It or Not

Only 9 Norwegians had settled in Minnesota Territory in 1850. By 1875, there would be over 80,000.[87]

Believe It or Not

Before the rise of the railroads, ox-pulled carts were the primary form of transportation over land in Minnesota. Three major ox-cart trails stretched across Minnesota. They ran west from St. Paul to the Red River valley and what is now North Dakota, then on to the Canadian border. Ox-carts fell out of use once the railroad arrived statewide, and most disappeared. Still, some segments of trail are still traveled quite often, as their former paths are now covered by highways or interstates.

THREE CITIES, NOT TWO

In just a few decades, Fort Snelling went from being the frontier to becoming something close to "civilization," and a number of cities quickly sprung up around it. Saint Paul, founded in 1840, and the town of Saint Anthony, founded in 1849, were among the first to be formally founded, and they quickly prospered due to proliferation of lumber mills and trade.[88, 89] Minneapolis wouldn't be officially founded until 1854, but it originally had a different name—Albion, which means "white" and refers to the chalky cliffs of Dover in England.[90, 91] That name mercifully didn't last; others considered were Brooklyn, Addiseville and Winona.[92] When Minneapolis— a combination of the Dakota word *Mni* (meaning waters) and the Greek word "polis" (meaning city)—was proposed in 1856, it was quickly adopted, though it was originally spelled Minnehapolis, with a silent "h."[93]

Believe It or Not

Perhaps the most cheeky name considered for early Minneapolis was All Saints, presumably in an attempt to one-up the two "saintly" cities that already existed in the area—Saint Paul and Saint Anthony.[94]

St. Paul in 1853

OTHER MISTRANSLATED PLACE NAMES

Minnehaha Falls isn't the only place with a garbled place name. To the Dakota, Mille Lacs Lake was known as *mde wákaŋ* (Spiritual/Mystic Lake), but it was later dubbed "Mille Lacs" by the French. This is a strange name, given that it literally means "thousand lakes" in French. The Rum River, which flows out of Mille Lacs, was also known as the "Spirit River," but a mistranslation caused "Spirit" to become "Rum." Recently, there has been a movement to restore the river's original name. Sometimes, "Indian-sounding" names were outright invented. Henry Schoolcraft, the first European to identify the Headwaters of the Mississippi, was somewhat notorious for making up names when naming counties in nearby Michigan. In all, he created over two dozen counties with nonsense names like Alcona, Alpena and Tuscola.[95]

1840s
1850s

Believe It or Not

In a famous billboard that once stood on the Red Lake Reservation, Nanabozho (the Ojibwe trickster god) saves the forests from Paul Bunyan by killing him with a giant walleye.[96] Sadly, vandals destroyed the sign.

Minnehaha Falls

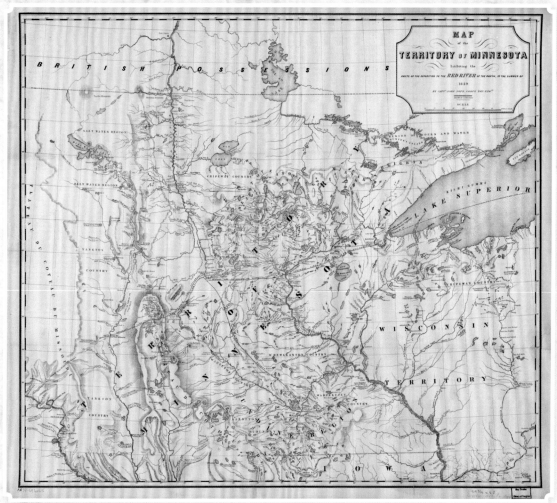

A map of Minnesota Territory

From Sawdust City to Flour Power (1850s – 1910s)

Before Minneapolis was known as the Flour Capital of the World, it was known as Sawdust City because of its many lumber mills. This period of time was an absolutely integral part of the state's history, as it involves everything from the U.S.-Dakota War of 1862 and Minnesota's involvement in the Civil War to the massive influx of European settlers and the taming (and harnessing) of St. Anthony Falls.

View of Minneapolis and St. Anthony in 1867

1850s
1860s

STATEHOOD AND THE ROAD TO THE CIVIL WAR

American Indian territories in 1858

By the end of the 1850s, Minnesota had changed a great deal; most of the land in present-day Minnesota had been ceded in treaties by American Indians, and settlers and commercial interests had begun moving into the state in earnest. The country was changing, too; states were being added fast and furious. From 1845–1865, *ten* states joined the Union—several during the Civil War, somewhat surprisingly.[1] Minnesota was among them, as were Iowa, Wisconsin, California and Texas. Minnesota was admitted to the Union on May 11, 1858.

Dred Scott

THE DRED SCOTT CASE, FORT SNELLING, AND MINNESOTA

Nonetheless, all was not well with the Republic, as the Civil War was just on the horizon. In fact, Minnesota's bid for statehood was held up for several months by a disagreement about whether or not future states would be allowed to hold a popular referendum to determine whether to become slave-holding states or not.[2] This debate essentially became moot with the Supreme Court decision in the Dred Scott case in 1857, which declared the Missouri Compromise (banning slavery in northern states) unconstitutional and deemed that African Americans remained slaves even if they visited states where slavery was illegal. That case centered around Dred Scott, a slave from Virginia. Scott had traveled to Minnesota—a slavery-free territory—with his owner,

1850s
1860s

Dr. John Emerson, the surgeon at Fort Snelling, living there for four years.[3] He sued for his freedom, arguing that he couldn't be a slave in a territory where slavery was illegal. After an initial trial in Missouri (where his owner had moved), a jury agreed that he should be freed, but the result was reversed on appeal. Eventually, Scott's case reached the Supreme Court; the timing couldn't have been more dramatic, as abolitionists were on the ascendancy and slavery was the issue of the day.

Believe It or Not

The quarters that Dred Scott likely shared with his wife are still present at Fort Snelling and can be toured. The quarters consist of a kitchen, as slaves were often expected to sleep where they worked.[4]

THE AFTERMATH AND THE PATH TO WAR

In an absolutely horrifying decision, the Supreme Court not only declared that Scott remained his owner's property, it also maintained that Scott didn't have a right to sue in open court, and denied that African-Americans could be citizens at all.[5, 6] The decision also invalidated the Missouri Compromise, which banned slavery in northern states. All of this infuriated the North and paved the way for war. Thankfully, Scott and his wife received their freedom after the decision, as they were transferred to an abolitionist owner. Dred Scott died just a year later, in 1858. His wife lived until 1877.

Believe It or Not

Dred Scott wasn't the only slave to visit Minnesota. Slavery existed on a small scale in Minnesota from the days of the fur trade, and even though it was formally outlawed, it continued even after the state was admitted to the Union. According to Professor Christopher Lehman at St. Cloud State University, there were as many as 20 slaves in Minnesota at a given time, most of them brought by southerners vacationing in Minnesota.[7]

THE FIRST TO SERVE

When the Civil War broke out in 1861, President Lincoln immediately put out a call for volunteers. Minnesota was the first state to offer troops to defend the Union and it also fielded the first volunteer regiment, the First Minnesota Volunteer Infantry, which would later play an incredibly important role at Gettysburg. In all, over 25,000 Minnesotans served on behalf of the Union, a pretty impressive total, given the state's population was only 170,000 in 1860.[8, 9] Many of Minnesota's troops were mustered early in the war (1861 and 1862), and they represented perhaps 10 to 12 percent of the state's 1860 population. By the end of the war, more than 2,500 Minnesotans were dead due to the war, most from disease. About 600 Minnesota soldiers died in combat.

A (very) idealized image of Union volunteers heading off to war

Believe It or Not

Minnesota's young men weren't the only ones to serve on behalf of Minnesota. African-Americans from Minnesota served in the war, as did many American Indians. One Minnesota woman even disguised herself as a man and managed to serve alongside her husband, until his death in battle.[10] Originally from Illinois, Frances Clalin lived on a farm in Minnesota and enlisted under the name Jack Williams, serving in a Missouri regiment. She was later discovered and discharged, returning to Minnesota before eventually heading east.

A NEW KIND OF WAR

Both sides expected the war to be a quick affair, but the first battle of the war—The First Battle of Bull Run (also known as The Battle of Manassas)—quickly dispelled those notions. There were nearly 5,000 casualties on a single day.[11] Military tactics were part of the problem. Tactics still resembled those of the Napoleonic Wars (soldiers walking abreast toward the opposing line), but technology, especially artillery, had advanced considerably, resulting in incredibly high casualties. Unfortunately, medicine had not kept pace with technology, and treatments were barbaric by contemporary standards. Anesthesia was a new technology, and while anesthetics were used, they weren't available everywhere.[12] Amputations were often used as a last resort.

Believe It or Not

The last surviving Civil War veteran from the Union was a Minnesotan.[13] Albert Woolson served as a drummer boy in the First Minnesota Heavy Artillery Regiment and died in Duluth in 1956 at the incredible age of 106.

WAR ON TWO FRONTS

Just as Minnesota was becoming accustomed to the grim progress of the Civil War, another war broke out, this one in Minnesota. In many respects, the U.S-Dakota War of 1862 was a long time coming. In just 50 years, the Dakota had been forced to cede nearly all of their land and abandon their traditional lifestyle, and the meager money and goods promised to them by treaties were funneled away, late or absent altogether.[14] With settlers flooding onto the plains and the Dakota's traditional foods in short supply due to overhunting, the Dakota were desperate and almost wholly dependent on the government for food.

Then, in July 1862, the government payments were late, and the local Indian Agent Thomas Galbraith refused to allow the Dakota to receive their food until the payments arrived. In a confrontation with the Dakota, Andrew Myrick, a trader and store owner, was asked what the Dakota were supposed to eat if they didn't receive the government food. He infamously responded that they could eat grass or their dung, as far as he was concerned.[15]

AN ATTACK LEADS TO WAR

Taoyateduta

The flashpoint that triggered the war took place on August 17, when a group of four Dakota killed five settlers in Acton Township. The Dakota warriors returned to their village and asked for help; there, a group of young soldiers asked Taoyateduta (Little Crow) to lead them in a battle against the settlers. Wary of the venture, he refused until he was called a coward. In a famous speech, he responded by predicting that a war against Europeans was futile and doomed to failure, but ended with, "Taoyateduta is not a coward; he will die with you."[16]

Believe It or Not

In his speech, Taoyateduta said that no matter how many whites the Dakota killed, there would be far more to replace them. The Census data at the time proves his point; in 1850, the population of Minnesota was just 5,000 people.[17] In 10 years, just before the start of the U.S-Dakota War, it was 170,000.

THE LOWER SIOUX AGENCY

Taoyateduta and his warriors attacked almost immediately, destroying the Lower Sioux Agency, where they killed 18 traders and government employees.[18] Among the dead was Andrew Myrick, the store owner who had said that the Dakota could eat grass. When his dead body was found, his mouth was filled with grass. After their success at the Lower Sioux Agency, Dakota warriors fanned out, attacking the farms and settlements that punctuated the countryside. More than 240 settlers were killed over the course of the next few days, and the

The Lower Sioux Agency Warehouse

1850s
1860s

Dakota took hundreds of hostages.[19] They also defeated a group of soldiers who had headed toward the Lower Sioux Agency from Fort Ridgely, killing over 20 U.S. Army regulars, the rest of whom retreated back to Fort Ridgely. In the interim, thousands of settlers fled east to safety.

Henry Sibley

ATTACKS ON FORT RIDGELY AND NEW ULM

The Dakota next attacked Fort Ridgely and New Ulm directly, attacking with hundreds of warriors. These attacks were unsuccessful, and New Ulm was subsequently evacuated.[20, 21] Early after the attacks, Governor Alexander Ramsey chose Henry Sibley to command a force to defeat the Dakota. The hastily assembled group of troops consisted of members of the U.S. Army, militiamen and volunteers.[22]

SLAUGHTER SLOUGH

Around the same time as the attacks on Fort Ridgely and New Ulm, a group of Dakota attacked a group of settlers near Lake Shetek, killing over a dozen and taking many hostage. Most of the dead were killed while attempting to hide in the long grass, giving the area the name of Slaughter Slough.[23] The hostages were eventually saved by a group of Lakota Indians who negotiated for their release. Known as "Fool Soldiers" because of Dakota animosity toward them, they put themselves at risk to save the settlers.[24]

Believe It or Not

The U.S.-Dakota War was a deadly affair. Minnesota lost somewhere between 400 and 800 civilians in the U.S-Dakota War. In the Civil War, Minnesota lost about 600 soldiers in combat, with about 2500 lost in all.

THE DAKOTA DEFEAT THE ARMY AT BIRCH COULEE

Sibley's forces slowly made their way in pursuit of Taoyateduta and the Dakota, and he sent out a group of soldiers to bury the bodies of settlers, which lay where they had fallen. This group of relatively green troops was ambushed, and nearly overrun altogether. In the end, 13 soldiers died and dozens were seriously wounded.[25]

THE BATTLE OF WOOD LAKE

After a series of small battles and an attack on Fort Abercrombie, Taoyat-eduta's forces met Sibley's in what would be the final battle of the war.[26] The Dakota planned to attack when Sibley's forces had broken camp and were marching in a column, where they would be easy pickings for several groups of Dakota, one of which was concealed in tall grass not far away from Sibley's camp. This plan, which may well have been successful had it been carried out, never came to fruition because a group of Sibley's soldiers headed out of camp (against orders) in search of potatoes.[27, 28] They headed directly toward some of the concealed Dakota, who opened fire, starting the battle prematurely. This left the Dakota in a precarious position, as most warriors were too far away to actually participate in the battle.[29] The Dakota were soundly defeated, and Taoyateduta retreated, disbanding the war party, effectively ending military action in the war.

Believe It or Not

At the Battle of Wood Lake, an errant search for potatoes determined the course of Minnesota history.

THE GRIM TOTAL

By the end of the war, hundreds of settlers were dead (there is no official count, though estimates usually put the total at 400–800), most of them civilians and a significant fraction of them children. Perhaps as many as 150 Dakota warriors died, and soon Sibley set up a military tribunal to try the Dakota responsible for the settler deaths.[30] By contemporary standards, it was a kangaroo court. Guilt by association was the rule of the day, and of the 393 indictments, 303 were convicted.[31] In the end, a whopping 77 percent of those indicted were sentenced to death.

1850s
1860s

A CONCENTRATION CAMP BY ANY STANDARD

Dakota non-combatants were punished as well. Nearly two thousand Dakota were forced to travel to a prison camp at Fort Snelling.[32] On the way, they were attacked by mobs, and many were injured or killed. The encampment at Fort Snelling was hardly a respite. Over the winter, perhaps as many as 300 Dakota died from disease, giving it a fatality rate of almost 20 percent.

THE LARGEST EXECUTION IN U.S. HISTORY

In a deeply unpopular move, President Abraham Lincoln commuted the death sentences of most of the convicted Dakota. The 38 others were hung simul-

The 1862 execution in Mankato

taneously on the day after Christmas in 1862. It was the largest mass execution in U.S. history. The bodies were buried in a mass grave, then secretly dug up to be used for medical research. One of the doctors who dissected one of the Dakota was Dr. William Mayo, founder of the Mayo Clinic.

NOT THE END OF WAR FOR THE DAKOTA

While the war for Minnesota settlers was essentially over after the Battle of Wood Lake, the government pursued the Dakota and other American Indians, including many who didn't even live in Minnesota, let alone have any part in the U.S.-Dakota War. Known as the "Punitive Expedition," the remaining Dakota were pushed westward and eventually forced onto reservations scattered throughout the region. In Minnesota, all treaties with the Dakota were canceled and the government's official policy was outright expulsion.[33, 34] Bounties for Indian scalps were even issued—with up to $200 being offered. There was a significant bounty on Taoyateduta's head as well. Discovered while foraging in Minnesota with his son, Taoyateduta was shot by a settler and his son. They collected a combined bounty of $575 for his death.

Sad but True

Unbelievably, Taoyateduta's scalp and skull were on public display at the Minnesota Historical Society until well into the twentieth century.[35] The Society eventually turned over the remains to his family, who properly buried them.

THE FIRST MINNESOTA AT GETTYSBURG: FIVE MINUTES THAT CHANGED HISTORY

When the U.S.-Dakota War came to an end, the Civil War continued to rage, and in July 1863, Minnesota soldiers would play a decisive role at Gettysburg. On the battle's second day, the 262 soldiers of the First Minnesota Volunteer Infantry, which had already seen heavy casualties in other battles of the war, found itself at Cemetery Ridge, a key point in the defense of the Union position. During the battle, most of the troops manning that ridge had moved to cover other areas, making the First Minnesota the only group protecting the

The First Minnesota at Gettysburg

area. Unfortunately for the First Minnesota, 1,600 Confederate soldiers were bearing down on them.[36] If the line hadn't held, the Confederates may have won the day. General Winfield Hancock knew that reinforcements were on the way, but they wouldn't get there for five minutes at least. Hancock quickly issued an almost unthinkable order to Colonel William Colvill: he pointed at the Alabama flag making its way up the hill and said, "See those colors? Take them."[37] Colvill's troops fixed bayonets and charged, even though they were outnumbered five to one. The tactic worked, as reinforcements arrived in time, but only about twenty percent of the troops would emerge unscathed.[38] Of the 262 soldiers who charged, 47 remained unhurt afterward. Hancock would later say, "There is no more gallant deed recorded in history."

Believe It or Not

On the next day of the battle, the remnants of the First Minnesota were sent to the center of the line—supposedly a safe place. They soon found themselves fighting off Pickett's Charge, where they lost about thirty percent of the soldiers who had survived the day before.[39] They repelled Pickett's charge only with another desperate charge of their own.

Believe It or Not

In the battle, the First Minnesota captured the flag of the 28th Virginia Infantry. Now housed at the Minnesota Historical Society, the state of Virginia threatened to sue for the flag's return, but state officials and the Minnesota Attorney General would have none of it.[40]

THE HOMESTEAD ACT AND THE PIONEER HEYDAY

By the end of the Civil War in 1865, Minnesota's soldiers returned to a very different state. The Dakota Indians were largely gone, and the population of the state was skyrocketing, thanks in part to the Homestead Act, which gave away free land to settlers, as long as they agreed to build a 12x14 dwelling on it, reside there and tend crops for five years.[41] The appeal of free land drew tens of thousands to Minnesota, many of them immigrants from Germany, Norway

750,000
Acres
Indian Land
Open to Settlers

Under homestead laws. Land lies in the Flathead Reservation, Montana; Coeur d' Alene Reservation, Idaho, and Spokane Reservation, Washington. Some of the choicest land in the Northwest is contained in these tracts. Some is agricultural land, some grazing land, and there is some very valuable fruit and timber land. Prices will range from $1.25 to $7.00 per acre.

Register July 15 to August 5

at Kalispell, Montana; Coeur d' Alene, Idaho, and Spokane, Wash., all reached by fast trains of the *Great Northern Railway.* Low round trip fares every day this summer. Stop over and register en route to the Alaska-Yukon-Pacific Exposition.

Send for illustrated book describing the country, and giving details about When, Where, and How to register. Enclose four cents for postage.

W. J. DUTCH,
District Passenger
Agent.

Fourth and Robert,
St. Paul.

GREAT NORTHERN RAILWAY

A Great Northern land advertisement; similar ads were seen in Minnesota

and Sweden. In all, there have been several waves of European immigrants. After the initial influx in the 1850s, another major wave (mostly from Germany, Norway and Sweden) arrived at the turn of the twentieth century.

Believe It or Not

Minnesota's appeal to settlers was bolstered by newspapers and publications that described Minnesota in colorful terms like "the Empire State of the Northwest," and "the New England of the West."[42] Minnesota's beauty was also memorialized by Henry Wadsworth Longfellow in his epic poem, "The Song of Hiawatha." Despite his association with Minnesota, Longfellow's book was something of an armchair epic. He never actually visited Minnesota.

Believe It or Not

Hilariously, in the original Homestead Act, the legislators neglected to specify that the dwelling had to be 12x14 *feet*, so some unscrupulous speculators built tiny 12x14-inch-long structures to "meet" the requirements of the bill.[43]

Believe It or Not

At first, many considered the prairie to be difficult farmland, in large part because cast iron plows had trouble breaking up the soil. A young blacksmith named John Deere invented a steel plow that was better equipped to handle the tough soil. It revolutionized life on the prairie and was known as the "plow that broke the prairie."

European Place Names in Minnesota

Minnesota has seen many waves of immigrants over the course of its history. The following are just a few of the Minnesota place names inspired by European settlers.

FRENCH

Belle Plaine means "beautiful prairie"

Bois Forte means "strong woods," and is a name the French gave the Indians living in the dense forests of the area[1]

Cloquet is a French surname; the origin is somewhat uncertain

Detroit Lakes comes from the word *détroit*, which means "strait," and referred to a section of a lake that looked narrow

Duluth is named for explorer Daniel Greysolon, Sieur Du Lhut

Embarrass comes from the French word *embarrass*, meaning "hinder with difficulties;" the name stemmed from the Embarrass River, which was difficult to canoe

Fond du Lac means the "head of the lake"

Frontenac was named for Louis de Buade de Frontenac, a Governor of New France, which is part of Canada today

Grand Marais means "great marsh"

Hennepin was named for Father Louis Hennepin, a French missionary

Lake Mille Lacs means "one thousand lakes"

LaSalle is named for explorer René-Robert Cavalier, Sieur de La Salle

Little Marais means "little marsh"

Marquette was named for Jacques Marquette, a French Jesuit missionary who explored the Mississippi

Nicollet was named for Joseph Nicollet, a French explorer who mapped the Headwaters region of the Mississippi

Roseau means "reed;" named for the many reeds found in the Roseau River

St. Cloud is named for a suburb of Paris, which was in turn named in honor of a saint: a sixth-century monk named Clodoald.

St. Louis (multiple) is named for King Louis

GERMAN

New Ulm is named for the ancient city of Ulm (and birthplace of Albert Einstein!)

Minnesota is also home to a number of cities and townships named for German towns and cities, including Cologne, Burleene (Berlin), Hanover, Hamburg, New Trier, Eitzen, Gotha, Germantown and, amazingly, even a New Germany.

FINNISH[III]

Finland is named in honor of the ancestral homeland of the Finnish immigrants who settled there

Finlayson is named for a prominent Finnish immigrant in the town[II]

Suomi means "Finland" in Finnish

Kalevala is named for the "Kalevala," widely regarded as Finland's national epic

Waasa is named for the province of Vaasa in Finland

Wuori means "mountain"

Salo is named for Salo, Finland

Alango is either a Finnish surname or a version of the word "lowland"[IV]

Toivola means "Hopeville"[V]

NORWAY

Many of the Norwegian place names refer to towns or districts in Norway. Examples include: Solem, Urness, Tofte, Hovland, Oslo, Westerheim, and several different versions of Norway Village or Township.[VI]

1870s
1890s

THE END OF THE FUR TRADE, THE BEGINNING OF BIG LUMBER

By the end of the Civil War, the fur trade in Minnesota was all but dead. Nonetheless, Minnesota's northern forests were relatively untouched by lumber interests, and lumber barons to the east would soon take note, leading to an economic boom that would utterly trans-form the state and its forests, and lead to the emergence of the Twin Cities as an economic power in the region.

Logging in Beltrami County in the early part of the twentieth century

Believe It or Not

Minnesota only had one ten-mile stretch of railroad until after the Civil War. Built in 1862, it linked St. Paul to St. Anthony.[44]

A log drive

THE TIMBER ERA

Just as the fur trade dominated Minnesota's economy in the eighteenth century, the nineteenth century would come to be dominated by lumber. The industry really took off after Minnesota became a territory in 1849, and by the time Minnesota became a state in 1858, the industry was growing exponentially, as lumber companies (and lumberjacks) began to flood into the state. In 1843, only

1.5 million board feet were cut statewide; by 1857, the total would be 44 million board feet. Amazingly, over two *billion* board feet of lumber were cut in 1899.[45]

Believe It or Not

A large white pine contained perhaps 2,000 board feet, and truly huge trees could produce up to 7000 feet of lumber, enough for perhaps two small ranch-style houses.[46, 47]

SOME HUGE TREES

The Minnesota DNR compiles a list of Minnesota's "Champion Trees"—the tallest of each species. Minnesota's current white pine, located in Fillmore County, is a whopping 103 feet tall and over 17 feet in circumference. And that's not anywhere near the tallest white pine recorded in the region. Records are spotty (as lumberjacks were more interested in cutting the tree down than comparing it to the rest), but some white pines in the region are much taller. The General MacArthur White Pine in Wisconsin, for instance, reached 130 feet tall, and at their tallest, truly incredible specimens probably exceeded 200 feet.[48, 49]

Believe It or Not

In exceptional cases, white pines can live up to 450 years, but that's nothing compared to the current record holder, a giant bristlecone pine in California.[50] It's reportedly 5,062 years old, making it (500 years!) older than the Great Pyramid of Giza.[51]

Believe It or Not

If the most extraordinary of the state's white pines topped out at 200 feet, it's likely that the state's tallest tree was taller than its tallest building until sometime around the turn of the twentieth century, when a number of buildings in excess of 200 feet were built, including Minneapolis City Hall (and its 300-foot clock tower).[52]

RIVER FLOATS AND LOG RAFTS

Given the incredible weight of the wood and the primitive state of the logging roads (a road was literally chopped out of the forest), moving logs overland was difficult and inefficient, even for draft animals. Until the arrival of the railroads, transporting the logs by water was much easier.

There were two basic ways to transport lumber: with a log drive or floating them in a huge structure called a "crib."

The Paul Bunyan statue in Akeley, MN

In a log drive, logs were floated pell-mell down the river and guided by a team of loggers (called river pigs) who ran on top of the logs. Not surprisingly, log drives were incredibly dangerous, as loggers could only prevent logjams by using long poles to move logs in problematic areas (like rapids).

If the river was wider and straighter, the logs were tied together in a "crib" (essentially a wood frame) and floated down the river. These cribs were usually 16 feet long, and could be lashed together to form a giant makeshift raft of logs. These rafts reached hundreds of feet long and were steered with oars by loggers—who lived on top of the rafts in primitive buildings.[53]

On wider rivers, like the Mississippi, log rafts became a constant sight, and logs were even floated all the way down to St. Louis. Sawmills and cities downstream were often the beneficiaries of this industry and major mills sprung up downstream at Stillwater and the Twin Cities. Such lumber towns boomed, and others sprung up once logging railroads were built, toward the close of the nineteenth century. Eventually, railroads made their way across the state, eventually making log rafts a thing of the past.

LUMBERJACK LINGO

Lumberjacks were colorful figures, and their work spawned its own vocabulary. Here's a selection of interesting logging terms, some of which have seeped into popular culture.

Deadhead: A log that has mostly sunk in a lake or river, leaving only a visible "head" above water

Flunkey: The person responsible for doing various errands in the morning, including waking up the men[I]

Frog eggs: Tapioca[II]

Gut robber: A lousy cook[III]

Haywire: A logging operation with shoddy equipment, as if held together by hay wire (baling wire)[IV]

Hungry jacks: Lumberjacks[V]

High and dry: When logs are floated downstream when water levels are too low, leaving the logs stuck on the river flats until the water level rises

Logjam: A group of logs that have gotten stuck in a jumble, often in a rapids. Logjams were incredibly dangerous for loggers and sometimes had to be freed with dynamite

Overland trout: Bacon[VI]

Skid row: A road where horses pull logs; also the area where loggers hang out when in town[VII]

Widowmaker: A dangerous hanging limb that can fall on unsuspecting loggers; the Argopelter was a legendary creature that was said to kill lumberjacks by throwing widowmakers on them[VIII]

LOGGING, NOT FORESTRY

Unfortunately, the lumberjacks were loggers—not foresters. Logging consists simply of cutting down logs, then moving on, with little concern for the forest. Forestry involves logging, but it is as concerned with resource management—enabling logging in the future. During the logging era, the virgin forests of Minnesota were deemed to be an inexhaustible resource, but in reality, they were almost entirely clear-cut within a hundred years.[54]

CLEAR-CUTTING LEADS TO FOREST FIRES

Clear-cutting had some serious consequences. For one, it greatly increased the likelihood of fire, as the cut-over land was often littered with downed limbs and other kindling. Several major forest fires struck Minnesota. The infamous Hinckley Fire of 1894 leveled the

Clear-cut land

entire town and burned hundreds of square miles, killing more than 400 people. Another major fire struck Cloquet in 1918, and it too killed more than 400 people.

Believe It or Not

The death toll in the Hinckley Fire would have been a lot higher were it not for the actions of many brave citizens. One of them, engineer James Root, arrived in town only to find it burning. People immediately began climbing aboard, and he ended up saving hundreds by driving his locomotive backwards, away from the flames, until the train reached the safety of a shallow lake. The fire was so hot the train started on fire and the heat broke the glass of the windows.

Believe It or Not

Located on Leech Lake, the town fathers named Walker, Minnesota, in honor of lumber baron Thomas B. Walker. Walker later founded the famous Walker Art Center. The original museum consisted of an additional room added to his house that he filled with paintings, and he let anyone come visit.[55]

Believe It or Not

The largest raft of logs floated down the Mississippi contained 5.5 million board feet of lumber.[56] The best virgin forests produced somewhere around 50,000 board feet of lumber per acre, so the trees in that raft probably originally covered something like 100 acres, making the raft the equivalent of a floating forest.[57]

MINNEAPOLIS BECOMES THE MILL CITY

Just as the lumber industry began to come into its own in the 1850s and 1860s, Minneapolis began to harness the power of St. Anthony Falls. Sawmills sprung up first, and prospered until the late 1880s, when flour mills followed suit.[58]

St. Anthony Falls

A HISTORY OF THE FALLS

Minneapolis became a metropolis because of ready access to waterpower, and in the Twin Cities, waterpower meant one thing—St. Anthony Falls. While we often think of waterfalls as being permanent landmarks, in a real respect, that's not true at all. In fact, waterfalls are always on the move.[59] They form when moving flows of water scour away the bedrock beneath them, creating an ever-steeper grade, and eventually, an outright falls. This process takes thousands of years, and it also means that waterfalls are always slowly retreating further and further upstream. St. Anthony Falls, for example, moved 10 miles over the first 12,000 years of its existence.[60]

THE FALLS FALL APART

Unfortunately, once St. Anthony Falls were harnessed for industry, the retreat of the falls accelerated. Part of the problem was the geology of the falls—the bedrock beneath it consists of limestone, a fairly weak rock, and the development of sawmills, and later the canals, dam and waterworks

1870s
—
1890s

that helped funnel water toward the city's mills, only accelerated the falls' retreat. In the sawmill era, rogue logs would often spill over the dam, crashing into the limestone and gouging out great chunks.[61] The construction of a V-shaped dam (to funnel the water to the mills on the east and west sides of the river) also left the middle of the falls high and dry, accelerating the destruction due to freezing and thawing cycles. Worse yet, the rock beneath the limestone was sandstone—a rock so soft you can literally break it with your hands.

THE TUNNEL DISASTER

The St. Anthony Falls were nearly destroyed in 1869, when a tunnel being built under the river collapsed, creating two whirlpools. While no one was

The Tunnel Disaster, 1869

hurt, residents on both sides of the river desperately attempted to fill them in using large rafts of timber; these attempts proved futile, as the rafts were later destroyed by the rushing water.[62] Eventually, the U.S. Army Corps of Engineers were called in, and after many failed attempts, they finally succeeded in building a 40-foot-deep, 1850-foot-long concrete wall beneath the falls themselves, protecting the falls from additional erosion.[63] The process was not quick, however; work on the wall and other structures (including several dams) wasn't finalized until the 1880s.

Believe It or Not

In their early days, 12,000 years ago, St. Anthony Falls were much bigger. Fueled by glacial meltwater, they were approximately 1,200 feet across and about 180 feet high.[64, 65]

1890s 1910s

BREAD FOR EVERYONE!

With the falls secured as a source of waterpower, Minneapolis boomed. By 1890, Minneapolis was producing more flour than any other city on the planet. At its peak in 1915–1916, Minneapolis produced 20,443,000 barrels.[66] A barrel held 196 pounds, so Minneapolis produced over four billion pounds of flour. Assuming that you need three cups of bread for one loaf of bread, that means Minneapolis produced enough flour to make over five *billion* loaves of bread, enough for two for every person on earth at that time.

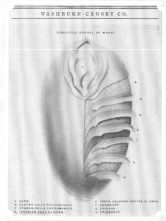

A wheat kernel diagram from a Washburn-Crosby publication

Famous Tycoons and Lumber Barons

In Minnesota, the late nineteenth century and the early twentieth century was the age of the tycoon. Even today, names like Pillsbury and Walker are familiar. Here are a few of the tycoons of the era, as well as some buildings and places associated with them today:

- James Jerome Hill, chief executive of the Great Northern Railway, known for his mansion, the James J. Hill library, and the Stone Arch Bridge, which he built

- Charles Alfred Pillsbury and John S. Pillsbury, founders of the Pillsbury Flour company, known for the Pillsbury House Theater, the Pillsbury Settlement House, and connections to the University of Minnesota

- Thomas Barlow Walker, owner of timber companies, known for the Walker Art gallery and his support of the public library system

- Thomas Lowry, founder of the Minneapolis Street Railway Company, known for Lowry Hill, the Lowry Tunnel, the Lowry Avenue Bridge, and Lowry Park[I]

1890s
1910s

- James Ford Bell, president and chairman of General Mills, known for the James Ford Bell Museum of Natural History, the James Bell House and the James Ford Bell Library at the University of Minnesota

- William Hood Dunwoody, partner of what would become General Mills; he was founder of Dunwoody Institute and benefactor of the Minneapolis Institute of Arts [II]

A PAIR OF GOLD RUSHES, AND THE RISE OF THE IRON RANGE

The California gold rush of 1849 is rightfully the most famous gold rush in U.S. history, but it was hardly alone. In fact, a pair of gold rushes in Minnesota profoundly changed the state's history. The first centered upon Lake Vermilion in northern Minnesota and occurred just after the Civil War in 1865–1866.[67] Not much gold was found, but more gold was found in a rush surrounding Rainy Lake, where a small mine was even established.[68] The most important discovery in these rushes wasn't gold at all—it was iron. In all, three distinct iron ranges were discovered: The Vermilion, the Mesabi and the Cuyuna Ranges. Companies soon formed to extract the ore around the turn of the twentieth century.

A TAPESTRY OF CULTURES

Just as German, Scandinavian and Irish immigrants had helped drive Minnesota's early development, Minnesota's mining boom owed much to another wave of immigrants, this time including immigrants from Finland, Croatia and Slovenia and a host of other European countries.[69, 70]

NEW TOWNS, BUT NOT ALWAYS A PERMANENT ADDRESS

These immigrants soon settled in places with names like Finland and Ironton and Kalevala and Mountain Iron and Taconite. Railroads, which already crisscrossed the state, soon connected the mines to the harbor at Duluth-Superior, and ore from Minnesota soon became the dominant source of iron nationwide, producing upwards of sixty percent of the country's supply.[71] Life for mining families was often difficult—with long hours, dangerous work and primitive accommodations.[72] On a few famous occasions, entire towns had to be moved altogether. This occurred several times, perhaps most famously in Hibbing, Minnesota. The town was found to reside atop seams of rich ore, so in 1919 the mining company began moving the entire town two miles in order to mine the iron beneath. To compensate the (literally) uprooted citizens, they built a lavish high school—which is absolutely incredible—as well as a massive city hall. Both are now on the National Register of Historic Places and sites to see.

Believe It or Not

To give you an idea of how opulent Hibbing High School is, its massive theater boasts three stages and has an incredibly rare pipe organ.[73] It's also lit by two huge chandeliers that cost $15,000 when originally constructed and are now insured at $250,000 each. The auditorium is also allegedly haunted; a spirit is claimed to inhabit one specific seat—J47.[74]

ORE YOU COULD WELD

The Vermilion Range was renowned for its incredibly high-quality ore— the original deposits often contained 50–60 percent iron, high enough that two pieces could be welded together.[75] [76] The Mesabi Range also had very high-quality ore, averaging somewhere around 50 percent. The Cuyuna Range's ore had more manganese in it, and it would soon become one of the primary sources of that metal during World War I.[77]

1890s 1910s

Believe It or Not

Mining wasn't without its risks. In the worst mine disaster in Minnesota history, 41 miners died when the Milford Mine flooded in 1924. Located near Crosby, the mine was an underground mine (unlike the open pit mines that are common now). It was situated between a pair of lakes. When one section of the mine caved in, a deluge of water and mud followed, killing the unsuspecting workers.

Trip to the General Store: Prices, Then and Now[I, II, III]

Remember when gasoline was $0.99 a gallon? Those were the days! Well, inflation isn't a new phenomenon. Prices for everyday items were much cheaper early in Minnesota's history. (Of course, incomes were much lower back then, too.) Still, it's fun to compare prices then and now. Here are some prices from a general store, circa 1914, compared with conservative estimates from modern-day shops.

Note: You don't see dresses, pants and suits on this list, as many households made their own clothes at home.

ITEM	PRICES IN 1914	NOW
Men's shoes	$2.98	$20
Ladies' shoes	$1.29	$20
Children's shoes	$0.69	$15
Handkerchiefs	$0.69	$2
Suspenders	$0.19	$13
Belts	$0.39	$20
Ties	$0.19	$10
Heavy Coat	$7.98	$80
Corsets	$0.49 to $1.89	$20
Hats	$0.79 to $2.29	$30
1 can peaches, apples, cherries or pears	$0.21	$1.72 (large can)
1 can beans, corn, peas or tomatoes	$0.07	$4 (large can)
1 lb. raisins	$0.11	$3

ITEM	PRICES IN 1914	NOW
1 lb. high-grade coffee	$0.25	$5.15
1 lb. dry tea	$0.45	$6.56
1 lb. rice	$0.07	$0.73
5 lbs. oats	$0.21	$9
½ sack of flour (50 pounds)	$1.50	$26

From World War I
to the Present Day
(1910s – present)

Minnesota's twentieth-century history serves as an excellent microcosm of
that of the nation's. Minnesotans played important roles in literature, aviation,
war and many other fields, and Minnesotans and Minnesota institutions
featured directly into major world events, positive and negative. From the
tarring and feathering of John Meintz during the anti-German craze during
World War I to Charles Lindbergh's famous flight and his fall from grace
during the run-up to World War II, the twentieth century saw Minnesota
begin entering the world stage in earnest.

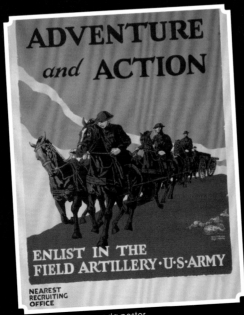

World War I propaganda poster

1910s
1920s

MINNESOTA INTO THE FIRST WORLD WAR

Because of its still-booming iron ore and mill industries, Minnesota played an especially important role in the war effort. The U.S. joined the war reluctantly in 1917 after several years of unrestricted submarine warfare, in which passenger liners carrying American citizens were sunk, including the famous *Lusitania*. In 1917, the U.S. also became aware of a proposed plot between Germany and Mexico that featured the infamous Zimmermann Telegram, a proposal sent by the Germans to entice Mexico to attack the U.S. if the U.S. entered the war on behalf of the allies. The Germans promised financial support and U.S. territory (including Texas), but Mexico demurred, as it knew it had no chance militarily and no real desire for war. This proved to be one of the final straws, and the U.S. soon joined the war.

THE ANTI-GERMAN CRAZE, THE HOME GUARD AND THE MINNESOTA COMMISSION OF PUBLIC SAFETY

While the U.S. may have been reluctant to join the war, an anti-German fervor soon developed and propaganda became commonplace. In 1917, the draconian Espionage Act was passed, and in 1918, the Sedition Act was passed; both were attempts to stifle dissent against the war, and in particular, to combat "agitation," whether by labor interests and unions or by "disloyal" citizens.[1] With over 117,000 citizens of German descent in Minnesota at the turn of the

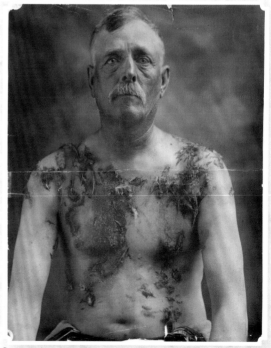

German-American citizen John Meintz after being tarred and feathered

century, those in power soon became concerned that Minnesotans of German descent might prove disloyal and attempt to combat industrial production.[2] Minnesota soon became a hotbed of anti-German sentiment, and the state passed a law creating "The Minnesota Commission of Public Safety," an organization granted broad powers to fight disloyalty and promote "patriotism."[3] Aliens in Minnesota were compelled to register with the state government and declare their property; these "civic slackers" (I'm quoting!) also had to explain why they hadn't become citizens.[4] Textbooks that weren't sufficiently patriotic were banned and "Germanic" art was taken down. A "Home Guard" of nearly 10,000 soldiers was established to maintain order—and especially to prevent strikes and quell any labor unrest. Anti-German feeling was so prominent that there were even physical attacks on German citizens in Minnesota. John Meintz, a farmer living near Luverne, Minnesota, was abducted, beaten, and tarred and feathered before being dumped in South Dakota. The assailants were all tried, but acquitted. The town's residents celebrated the acquittal. Many other Minnesotans of German descent were accosted and forced to kiss the American flag.[5]

Believe It or Not

If Minnesota's Public Safety Commission sounds familiar, it should. During the French Revolution, the Committee of Public Safety was formed to combat "anti-revolutionaries." In the Reign of Terror that followed, tens of thousands of "disloyal" citizens were guillotined or summarily executed. Victims included King Louis XVI, Marie Antoinette, the famous chemist Lavoisier and eventually, one of the leaders of the Committee of Public Safety, Maximilien Robespierre himself.

Believe It or Not

An issue of the Public Safety Commission's newspaper had a headline that blared, "One Country, One Flag, One People and One Speech."[6] Ironically, the phrasing and sentiment were hardly different from a very similar German message in the 1940s—*ein Reich, ein Volk, ein Führer* (one kingdom, one people, one leader).

Brewing in Minnesota

With legions of German immigrants, it's not surprising that Minnesota has a long brewing history. Hundreds of breweries have been established in the state since European settlement. Some of them—such as Schell's—are still going, and this long tradition continues today with dozens of newer establishments. Here's a look back at just a few of Minnesota's most historic—and famous—breweries.

AUGUST SCHELL BREWING COMPANY

Founded by a pair of German immigrants in 1860, August Schell's Brewery is nearly as old as Minnesota itself, and it has survived the U.S.-Dakota War, Prohibition and a host of financial difficulties in the 1950s and '60s, when the widespread adoption of aluminum cans and mobile refrigeration made small breweries less competitive, leading many breweries to close. Schell's nearly closed its doors, but was saved after a large walnut tree on the brewery's grounds was cut down and sold for lumber.[I] (The tree had been planted by August Schell himself.) Today the company is widely known for its variety of craft beers, including a number of award-winners.

THEODORE HAMM BREWING COMPANY

The Theodore Hamm Brewing Company was founded in 1865 and operated in Minnesota for more than a century, eventually becoming one of the largest breweries in the country.[II] Unfortunately, the company suffered due to competition from larger breweries like Anheuser-Busch, and it was eventually sold a number of times. This first sale was the start of a downward spiral. Today, Hamm's beer is still made—the brand is owned by CoorsMiller—but it is no longer made in Minnesota.

Of course, any discussion of Hamm's would be incomplete without a mention of two things: baseball and the Hamm's Bear. Hamm's was one of the most important sponsors of the early Minnesota Twins franchise. Not only did they help bring the team to the state, their ads were common fixtures in between innings. Hamm's ads became famous nationwide in 1952, when the Hamm's Bear was first introduced. The ads featured an animated bear and the company's famous jingle, "From the land of sky-blue waters . . ."

1910s
1920s

Those ultra-pure waters weren't just a selling point; since the demise of the brewery and its subsequent abandonment, the well on-site is now used by Urban Organics to raise fish, which in turn, provide food for plants. Such "aquaponics" facilities can produce food year-round.[III]

MINNEAPOLIS BREWING COMPANY

A consolidation of a number of smaller breweries, the Minneapolis Brewing Company was created in an attempt to stave off competition from breweries based outside of Minnesota.[IV] The Minneapolis Brewing Company is most famous for its Grain Belt brand of beer, which was first released in 1893 and has been known as "The Friendly Beer" since 1933. After beer production at the company was shuttered by Prohibition, Grain Belt was released again once Prohibition ended, and the company survived until the 1970s. With the closure of the Minneapolis Brewing Company, the future of Grain Belt was in jeopardy, and production of Grain Belt eventually left the state after the label was purchased, before returning under the auspices of a new company, Minnesota Brewing. That company eventually failed as well, and that's when the August Schell Company stepped in, purchasing the rights to make Grain Belt, which it has done ever since, even launching Grain Belt Nordeast, in honor of the beer's heritage in Northeast Minneapolis.

FITGER'S

A Duluth landmark, the Fitger's Brewery building was the site of Duluth's most prominent brewery for 115 years.[V] The brewery, which closed in 1972, has since been re-purposed as a hotel and retail complex, and it is now home to the Fitger's microbrewery.

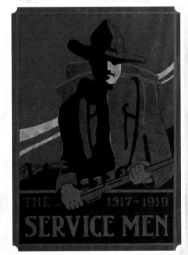

From a commemorative album of Waseca County, MN, soldiers in World War I

MINNESOTANS IN THE FIRST WORLD WAR

While the U.S. was only in the war for a relatively short time, it sent a staggering 2,000,000 troops overseas, with more than 116,000 killed in action. Minnesota sent

118,000 troops overseas and they paid a heavy price; in *Soldiers of the Great War*, a three-volume edition of U.S. soldiers killed in the war, there are eight pages (in tiny font) of Minnesota soldiers who died in action or of disease.[7, 8]

SUFFRAGE IN MINNESOTA

A different sort of war was raging while Minnesotans fought in the forests of France: Minnesota women were fighting for the right to vote.[9, 10] The

A program from a woman suffrage procession in 1913

Minnesota Woman Suffrage Association (known today as the Minnesota League of Women Voters) urged state lawmakers to pass women's suffrage, but these bills were voted down on a number of occasions.[11] Eventually, Minnesota did ratify the Nineteenth Amendment—the fifteenth state to do so—and women officially gained the right to vote when Tennessee ratified the amendment on August 18, 1920. Some Minnesota women could hardly wait to vote. A group of women in South St. Paul organized a local vote the next day, becoming the first women to vote after ratification of the Nineteenth Amendment.[12]

Believe It or Not

Constitutional amendments must be ratified by three-fourths of the states, and when the Nineteenth Amendment went into effect, a full one-fourth of the states hadn't ratified the Amendment. The last state to ratify the Amendment, Mississippi, didn't ratify it until 1984.

1910s
1920s

MINNESOTA'S PROHIBITION CONNECTION

Minnesota played an important part in another Constitutional Amendment—the Eighteenth, which enacted Prohibition, banning the production, sale and transport of alcoholic drinks.[13] The Amendment was purposely vague, as it didn't actually ban alcohol consumption or even specify what constituted an alcoholic beverage. To clarify this, Congress was expected to step in, and the Volstead Act, named for Minnesota politician Andrew Volstead, soon became the law of land. Hailing from Kenyon, Minnesota, (and later Granite Falls) Volstead didn't actually write all of the bill; instead, it was heavily influenced by Wayne Wheeler, the leader of the Anti-Saloon League.[14] By any measure, the Volstead Act was a disaster. The law contained a baffling array of loopholes. Consumption of previously stored liquors wasn't actually illegal, and citizens could legally consume liquor that they obtained for other reasons, including liquor received with a prescription.

Believe It or Not

Many bootleggers brought alcohol over the border from Canada. Bizarrely, the U.S. once developed a contingency plan for invading Canada.[15] Created in the 1920s, the plan was updated several times, before being publicly declassified in the 1970s. Called War Plan Red, it envisioned an invasion of Canada in a theoretical war with Britain. The plan called for annexing all of the British possessions in the hemisphere. Around the same time, Canada promulgated its own plan (for a counterattack); called Defence Scheme 1, it envisioned attacks on Fargo and Grand Forks, then Minneapolis and attacks on the East Coast.[16]

THE ROARING TWENTIES

After the Volstead Act shuttered legitimate alcohol makers, bootlegging became incredibly common. In the cities, large criminal cartels sprung up to meet the soaring demand, resulting in the likes of Al Capone and Bugs Moran in Chicago. In the end, the law did more to alter liquor production than actual consumption. Minnesota was profoundly affected by Prohibition, as speakeasies, gangsters and bootleggers were found throughout the state.

Believe It or Not

In the early twentieth century, Saint Paul was a safe-haven for criminals thanks to the informal "O'Connor" system. Established by Chief of Police John O'Connor, the system allowed criminals to stay in the area as long as they checked in with police, didn't commit crimes in the city and, perhaps most importantly, paid police a bribe.

A Brief Crime Tour of Minnesota

The Twin Cities were once criminal havens, especially for the Irish and Italian mobs. This was especially true in the 1920s and '30s, when the list of criminals that visited the state was a veritable Who's-Who of baddies, including Al Capone, John Dillinger, Alvin Karpis, The Barker Gang, Machine Gun Kelly, and George Babyface Nelson. Many of the sites where these criminals committed their dastardly deeds are still present today.

MANKATO EXECUTION SITE

Most of Minnesota's famous crimes consist of bank heists or mob hits, but Minnesota is home to a sad record: it was home to the largest mass execution in U.S. history. After the Dakota were defeated in the U.S.-Dakota War of 1862, a conflict that killed hundreds on both sides, authorities quickly set about punishing the Dakota. To do so, they detained and tried hundreds of Dakota men in military tribunals. The trials, such as they were, were short, speedy, conducted in English (which many Dakota didn't speak), and the defendants had no legal representation. It was essentially a kangaroo court. In the end, the trials resulted in death sentences for 303 Dakota men. President Lincoln commuted most of these offenses, leaving 39 death sentences intact. One prisoner was spared at the last minute, but the other 38 men were hung en masse in Mankato on the day after Christmas in 1862. Historical research indicates that at least one innocent man was hung that day (in part because of a similar-sounding name).[I] Today the execution site is known as Reconciliation Park.

JESSE JAMES IN NORTHFIELD, MINNESOTA

On September 7, 1876, Jesse James and the James-Younger gang—eight men strong—attempted to rob the First National Bank of Northfield.[II] The robbery went awry almost from the start. The three would-be robbers inside failed to obtain much cash thanks to Joseph Heywood, a bank teller and

1910s
1920s

former Union soldier who refused to open the safe (and even attempted to trap one of the bandits in a vault). Outside, the five other members of the gang soon found themselves under fire, as the citizens had sounded the alarm and armed themselves. Soon, two gang members were killed, and the rest were injured, some severely: Bob Younger was shot a total of 11 times. The gang split up; the Younger Gang was soon captured (and one more member was killed) and sent to prison. The James Brothers escaped and evaded capture; Jesse James was later shot by an associate looking for a reward. Frank James was later tried and acquitted for several previous crimes, but he was never tried for the Northfield Raid.

SITE OF THE FIRST CAR BOMBING IN MINNESOTA— AND PERHAPS THE WORLD[III]
Address: 1607 7th Street West, St. Paul

If you were a criminal in St. Paul in the 1920s, you knew "Dapper" Danny Hogan. The boss of the area's Irish Mob, Hogan was essentially in charge of the St. Paul underworld and got his nickname for his stylish clothes. As far as criminals go, Hogan was a well-respected figure, thanks to his reputed generosity to locals. Unfortunately for Hogan, his criminal empire became too lucrative, and someone wanted to take it over. They did so by planting a car bomb beneath the floorboards of Hogan's Paige coupe; the bomb detonated when Hogan tried to start the car, nearly severing his leg. He survived the surgery that amputated his leg, but soon fell into a coma and died the day of the attack. After word got out about his injury, dozens of well-known figures (including some police) showed up to offer blood transfusions.[IV] The culprits were never found, though it's suspected that Harry Sawyer, one of Hogan's associates, placed the bomb in order to inherit Hogan's criminal empire. This was one of the first car bombings in U.S. history (perhaps the first) and one of the first worldwide.

JOHN DILLINGER'S SHOOTOUT WITH THE FBI AND POLICE
Address: Lincoln Court Apartments, 95 Lexington Pkwy S, St. Paul

John Dillinger didn't stay in Minnesota for long (just about a month in 1933), but he sure made the news when he did.[V] In between bank robberies in the Midwest, Dillinger hid out with Evelyn "Billie" Frechette, in Apartment 303 of the Lincoln Court Apartments. FBI agents and St. Paul Police were tipped off to a pair of suspicious residents—but they didn't expect to find Dillinger and Frechette. A shootout ensued, and Dillinger and Frechette managed to escape because no one had thought to guard the back door.

BABY FACE NELSON ROBBED BRAINERD'S FIRST NATIONAL BANK IN BRAINERD[VI]

Address: S 6th St & Front Street, Brainerd

No longer the site of a bank, the old First National Bank building still stands in Brainerd, and it was the site of a robbery on October 27, 1933.[VII] The heist was led by Baby Face Nelson and netted thirty grand. The gang left behind some "souvenirs"—bullet holes. Nelson and his gang sprayed the building with gunfire as they left. Thankfully, no one was hurt.

Believe It or Not

Somewhat amazingly, when radio broadcasting began in St. Paul, the radio station KSTP would interrupt its regular programming to serve as a makeshift dispatch for the St. Paul Police.[VIII] The dispatcher interrupted the radio broadcast, sounded a gong, and then read the call to police.

Count Ferdinand von Zeppelin

THE END OF TWO ERAS BUT THE BEGINNING OF ANOTHER: FLIGHT

In Minnesota, the first two decades of the century were a time of transition—by the middle of the 1920s, the lumber industry was all but dead, and Minneapolis would lose its title as breadbox of the nation by the 1930s, with most mills being abandoned or demolished by the 1940s and 1950s. But Minnesota would play an important role in another field—aviation. Minnesota's first flights were balloon flights. The first balloon flight in Minnesota occurred in 1857. A few years later, in 1863, Count Ferdinand von Zeppelin—later the inventor of the rigid airship—made his first ascent in a balloon while in St. Paul.[17, 18] He later credited this trip with inspiring him to build his famous airships. The most

1910s
1920s

famous Zeppelin, the *Hindenburg,* burst into flames in New Jersey in 1937. The disaster was caught on film and captured on a radio broadcast narrated by Herbert Morrison, who famously exclaimed "Oh, the humanity!" as the burning ship came crashing down, killing 36 people.

Believe It or Not

On his trip to Minnesota, Zeppelin accompanied a small party on a trip up the Mississippi River.[19] The group, which quickly ran out of food, eventually had to resort to eating musk-rats. Worse yet, they had to eat them raw, as they had no way to make a fire.

MINNESOTA'S FIRST FLIGHTS

Aviation pioneer
Glenn Curtiss

The first powered flights in Minnesota didn't come until 1909 and 1910; the Wright brothers had succeeded in achieving powered flight in 1903, and once word got out about their achievement, aviation-mania soon spread worldwide.[20, 21] Because there were no airplane manufacturers at the time, would-be aviators had to build their own aircraft, and many people, including some Minnesotans, attempted to do that. Many of these designs were entirely divorced from any understanding of physics and consequently never made it into the air. A few did make short "hops" that hardly qualified as powered flight. The first successful flight in Minnesota probably occurred when Oliver Rosto built a replica of a French airplane and flew it in Duluth in 1909. A much bigger event occurred in 1910, when Minnesota held the "Twin City Aviation Meet" at the State Fairgrounds.[22, 23] It was a major event, featuring some of the more famous pilots in the world, including Glenn Curtiss, an aircraft-designer pilot who is widely considered the father of naval aviation. Curtiss was also famous for his 1907 land speed record of 136.4 miles per hour, which he set on a motorcycle equipped with a V8 engine.[24] (Aircraft, which were relatively slow compared to motorcycles and automobiles, wouldn't exceed that speed for about a decade.[25]) Conditions for flying were not ideal (it was blistering hot with very gusty winds), but Curtiss managed to put on a show nonetheless, and Minnesota would soon host a number of other aviation meets and barnstorming tours.

Believe It or Not

The engines on early aircraft were so unreliable that pilots often shipped their aircraft by train rather than fly them.[26] Still, being a pilot was so dangerous that planes were often damaged even on "successful" flights.[27]

1920s
1930s

Believe It or Not

One of the most famous early pilots in Minnesota was named Charles "Speed" Holman. A champion motorcycle racer, he soon became a pilot, and was perhaps best known for completing more than 1,400 consecutive loop-the-loops on one flight.[28] He died just a few years later in an airshow accident, and St. Paul's Holman Field is named for him.

AIR MAIL, THEN AIR COMMERCE

For the first decade or so of powered flight in Minnesota, barnstorming and air shows were the extent of the aviation industry. Eventually, the U.S. Post Office began experimenting with transporting mail by air.[29] (Due to the low speed and primitive accommodations on planes of the era—not to mention the danger of flying—reliable passenger service came much later in Minnesota.)

Believe It or Not

Being an Air Mail pilot was incredibly dangerous. Pilots died at the rate of about one a month.[30]

1920s
1930s

LUCKY LINDY

Charles Lindbergh, the most famous name in Minnesota aviation history, got his start as a barnstormer and, later, an Air Mail pilot. Lindbergh stunned the world in 1927 by successfully flying from Long Island to Paris, France, thereby claiming the $25,000 Orteig Prize. Raised in Little Falls, Minnesota, Lindbergh was considered a skilled pilot by his peers but was unknown on the world stage. He was not a favorite to claim the prize, especially given that he was facing some of the best pilots in the world at that time, including a number of World War I aces and naval pilots. Attempting the

Charles Lindbergh and the *Spirit of St. Louis*

crossing was incredibly dangerous, and this became clear as several of his competitors' attempts ended in disaster. Two weeks before Lindbergh's famous flight, two French World War I aces (Charles Nungesser and Francois Coli) had taken off from Paris in their plane, dubbed *The White Bird*, in an attempt to claim the prize.[31] They were spotted over Ireland and were never seen again; their fate remains one of aviation's great mysteries.

THE FAMOUS FLIGHT

Lindbergh's famous flight almost ended as quickly as it got started. His heavily loaded plane, the *Spirit of St. Louis*, was carrying 450 gallons of fuel and almost didn't clear telephone wires at the end of the runway.[32] In order to make his plane as light as possible, he removed all the excess weight he could. His plane didn't have lights, a parachute or a gas gauge.[33] He even cut out the portions of his maps that he wouldn't need. Once his flight was underway, sleep and navigation were Lindbergh's main foes. Flying with primitive navigational equipment and at the mercy of the winds, Lindbergh fought drowsiness for much of the flight, even falling asleep at one point on the 33-hour-long voyage. [34]

AN OVERNIGHT CELEBRITY

Charles Lindbergh

When Lindbergh arrived in Paris, he instantly became one of the most famous people in the world. About 100,000 people were waiting for him when he landed.[35] The technical achievement was staggering: controlled flight was in its infancy some 20-odd years before. Orville Wright's first flight only covered 120 feet. Lindbergh's covered over 3500 miles. In a respect, Lindy's feat was similar to Yuri Gagarin's launch into space or the Apollo 11 moon landing.

Believe It or Not

In 1944, Orville Wright was welcomed as a guest aboard a Lockheed Constellation, a then-state-of-the-art passenger plane that had just shattered speed and distance records in the aviation industry. Wright even flew the plane for a short period.[36] The Lockheed's wingspan exceeded the length of Wright's original flight.[37]

WHISKEY RUNNING AND COMMERCIAL SERVICE

The first iteration of Air Mail service in Minnesota was short-lived. Due to well-publicized crashes and budget cuts, the Minneapolis-to-Chicago Air Mail route was canceled. While planes were occasionally used to smuggle whiskey in from Canada, commercial air transportation wouldn't be permanently established in Minnesota until the formation of Northwest Airways in 1926, which ran a Chicago-to-Minneapolis mail route.[38] The company,

**1920s
1930s**

soon to be renamed Northwest Airlines (and later Northwest Orient Airlines), would dominate the aviation industry in Minnesota for the better part of the century.[39] An international carrier, it provided non-stop service to destinations worldwide, with many flights to the Pacific region. Northwest came to something of an ugly end. Attempting to cut costs, it saw its mechanics and ground crews go on strike in 2005, declared bankruptcy the same year, and eventually merged with Delta in 2008.[40] In the process, over 1,600 workers lost their jobs, including many who had been with the company for decades.

A Brief Walking Tour of F. Scott Fitzgerald's St. Paul[i]

The Roaring Twenties were a glamorous decade in the U.S., and in Minnesota. F. Scott Fitzgerald is one of the icons from that decade; one of Minnesota's most famous literary sons, Fitzgerald is as known for his wild lifestyle as he is for his works. Fitzgerald became famous after publishing his first novel, *This Side of Paradise* in 1920. His short stories soon became common fixtures in national magazines, and his novel, *The Great Gatsby* (published in 1925), is considered one of the finest novels ever written by an American.

Born in St. Paul on September 24, 1896, Francis Scott Key Fitzgerald lived in Minnesota (but especially St. Paul) on a number of different occasions during his life, and many of the structures he lived in are still standing and can be seen on the short walking tour listed below. [ii] When F. Scott Fitzgerald was young, his family suffered from financial difficulties. When they were in St. Paul, they moved almost constantly, living in many different houses and apartment buildings. Scott would repeat this pattern when he returned as an adult from 1919–1921.

Note: To make this walking tour easier to follow, these buildings are not listed in chronological order. All structures are located in St. Paul; please note that none of them are open for public tours.

Distance: About 1.3 miles.

481 LAUREL AVENUE, F. SCOTT FITZGERALD'S BIRTHPLACE.
A set of two buildings, F. Scott Fitzgerald was born on the second floor of the building on the left.

Directions: Head west about 200 feet to Mackubin Street, and turn left onto it. Two blocks later, take a right onto Holly Avenue.

509/514 HOLLY AVENUE
Fitzgerald lived in several buildings on this block of Holly Avenue at one point. The building at 509 Holly is an apartment building where the family stayed; they also lived in the house at 514 Holly. Scott lived on this block during his formative years, and it was this St. Paul atmosphere that figured into many of his later works.[III]

Directions: Walk down Holly Avenue until you reach Kent Street. Turn left onto Kent Street, and walk for two blocks until you reach Summit Avenue. Turn right onto Summit.

593/599 SUMMIT AVENUE
After struggling at Princeton, Fitzgerald joined the Army, where he was eventually stationed in Alabama, where he met his future wife, Zelda. After getting engaged to Zelda, who then broke off the engagement, he returned to Minnesota to live with his parents, where he wrote *This Side of Paradise*, his first novel. His parents lived in two different apartments in this large building.

Directions: From here, walk down Summit, until you reach Dale Street. Take a right onto Dale Street.

25 NORTH DALE
This is the site of the former St. Paul Academy, a private school that Scott attended. (There's now a Fitzgerald sculpture commemorating him.) For a writer of international renown, Fitzgerald wasn't a particularly good student. In particular, he was notoriously bad at spelling.

Directions: The former school site will be on your left-hand side in about half a block. After viewing it, head north. You'll meet Holly Avenue. Take a right and walk for about half a mile until you reach Western Avenue. Take a left.

COMMODORE BUILDING, 76 WESTERN AVENUE NORTH
This massive building, once known as the Commodore Hotel, is now a series of apartment buildings. This is where Fitzgerald and his wife lived when their only child, Frances Scott Fitzgerald, was born in 1921. The hotel was later popular with the underworld; John Dillinger also visited here later, as did Al Capone.[IV]

Directions: Walk two blocks north and you'll reach Laurel Avenue, where the tour started. Take a left to head back toward 481 Laurel Avenue.

THE GREAT DEPRESSION IN MINNESOTA

Lindbergh's flight was just a couple years removed from the stock market crash of 1929. While the crash didn't cause the Great Depression directly (the U.S. was already in recession in 1929), it helped turn recession into an outright depression.[41] The Depression occurred in large part because consumer spending fell off a cliff, leading to huge business losses and subsequent financial panics, which in turn led to massive increases in the unemployment rate nationwide. At the height of the Depression, the unemployment rate hit 25 percent. Minnesota was certainly not immune. To give you an idea of how bad things got, Hennepin County's population was 517,785 in 1930, and in 1933, over 120,000 people in the county needed assistance with food and shelter to survive.[42, 43] Thankfully, the various state and federal relief programs helped stave off outright starvation for most. Still, malnutrition was widespread and cases of starvation weren't unheard of.[44]

THE NEW DEAL IN MINNESOTA

When Franklin Delano Roosevelt was sworn into office in 1933, he quickly set about establishing a series of federal programs to provide employment opportunities for the struggling population. Two programs in particular had an important impact on Minnesota. The Works Progress Administration, built roads, bridges and infrastructure and hired cultural workers to produce books, art and host cultural events. The Civilian Conversation Corps hired

A Works Progress Administration poster

young, unmarried men for manual labor and construction projects through-out the state. Both left a very visible impact on Minnesota. If you've ever visited a state park, you've almost certainly benefited from the CCC, as they constructed many of the structures at Minnesota's state parks, and in some cases (such as Gooseberry Falls) developed the park almost from scratch. The CCC also built roads, blazed trails, drained swamps and planted millions of trees.[45] Nationwide, the statistics are staggering: All in all, the CCC employed over 3,000,000 men and they built over 125,000 miles of road, planted per-haps 3 billion trees and built 800 state parks.[46]

The Foshay Tower

MINNEAPOLIS AND ITS FIRST SKYSCRAPER: THE FOSHAY TOWER

Modeled after the Washington Monu-ment, the Foshay Tower is now a relatively diminutive building in down-town Minneapolis, but for four decades, it towered over the skyline.[47] Financed by Wilbur Foshay and built in 1929, it's a relic of the Roaring Twenties, and the building's official opening was a three-day spectacle in keeping with something out of an F. Scott Fitzgerald short sto-ry.[48] There were fireworks, dancers, and John Philip Sousa was even on hand to perform a piece he'd been commissioned to write specifically for the tower, "The Foshay Tower—Washington Memorial March." While the Foshay's opening was a success, Foshay's life quickly unraveled. Foshay made his money on the stock market, which had crashed on October 29. Crash or not, Wilbur Foshay must have known he was in trouble because he was soon convicted of running a pyramid scheme and sentenced to prison.

Believe It or Not

After the grand opening of the building, John Philip Sousa went to cash the $20,000 check he received from Foshay. It bounced.

THE RUN-UP TO WAR: ISOLATIONISM AND LINDBERGH

As the Great Depression slogged on, Hitler came into power in 1933, and soon it became clear that war was looming in Europe. With the horrors of World War I fresh on their minds, many in America didn't want to join another European war. The isolationist America First Committee formed in 1940 in an attempt to keep the U.S. out of the war, and its most famous spokesman was none other than Charles Lindbergh. Lindbergh had spent a considerable amount of time overseas, and he'd visited Germany during the 1936 Olympics, where he'd been a guest of honor of Hermann Göring, the leader of the Luftwaffe. After the Olympics, he was given a German medal by Göring, and he even planned on moving to Germany after the infamous kidnapping of his son.[49] Lindbergh also espoused racial views that certainly seemed sympathetic to those of the Nazis.[50] In an infamous speech given two months prior to the attack on Pearl Harbor, he blamed the push for war on three groups: the Jews, the British and the Roosevelt Administration.[51, 52] Given the infamy of Kristallnacht in 1938 and the reports of Nazi atrocities that were filtering back to the U.S., Lindbergh was intensely criticized for his speech. The isolationist movement, never all that popular to begin with, vanished after the Japanese attack on Pearl Harbor in 1941. Over the course of a little more than a decade, Lindbergh went from a world hero to something close to a pariah.

HOMEGROWN FASCISTS

Lindbergh wasn't alone in his sympathies for fascism (or at the very least, his admiration for Nazi Germany).[53] In the 1930s and 1940s Minnesota was infamous as a hotbed of anti-Semitism. Jews were unofficially barred from work in state government, and employment opportunities for Jews were next to non-existent.[54] Worse yet, there were an alarming number of homegrown

1930s — 1940s

fascists in the states. Most belonged to the Silver Legion, a national organization nicknamed the Silver Shirts because of the color of their uniforms, which emulated the foot soldiers of fascism in Europe: the Brown Shirts in Germany and the Black Shirts in Italy.

JEWISH MOBSTERS VS. MINNESOTA FASCISTS

In 1936, the Silver Shirts began holding meetings in Minnesota. An exposé in *The Minnesota Journal* by none other than Eric Sevareid (the famous newscaster and author of the Minnesota classic *Canoeing with the Cree*) brought the group to the public's attention. David "Davie the Jew" Berman, one of the leading mobsters in the Twin Cities, took note, and when he heard of a planned Silver Shirt meeting in the Twin Cities, he and his associates crashed the party and knocked some heads.[55] After Berman and his associates broke up a few other meetings in a similar fashion, the Silver Shirts weren't seen in the Twin Cities again.

Believe It or Not

A fascinating character, Berman's efforts against fascism didn't end with his victory over the Silver Shirts. Enraged about the plight of Jews in Europe, he tried to enlist in the U.S. military, only to be turned down because he was a felon. Undeterred, he went to Canada, where he enlisted in the 18th (Manitoba) Armoured Car Regiment, fighting in Europe.[56] After the war, he picked up right where he left off, moving to Las Vegas, where he helped found the Flamingo Casino with Bugsy Siegel. After Siegel's assassination by the mob, Berman became one of the major players in Las Vegas. David Berman died during a medical procedure, but his wife and daughter both died under odd circumstances. His wife died after an overdose of barbiturates, and his daughter, once a "princess of Las Vegas" who later became a successful writer and journalist, was killed in an execution-style hit in Las Vegas in 2000.[57] The case remains unsolved.

A modern-day photo of the Flamingo

WORLD WAR II, MINNESOTA AND FORT SNELLING

1930s
1940s

Once the war was underway, Minnesota quickly transitioned to a war footing. Fort Snelling became a regional center for induction into the Armed Forces. During the war, over 300,000 troops were medically screened, given qualification tests, assigned to units, given equipment and then sent along to other bases for basic training.[58] True to our Lake Wobegon roots, Minnesota's recruits fared better than average, and many of these higher-scoring recruits were assigned to the Army Air Corps.[59] Fort Snelling wasn't Minnesota's only contribution to the war effort. The U.S. military built the Twin City Ordinance Plant (later known as The Twin Cities Arsenal). It was operated by Federal Cartridge Company, which is still around today. During the war, the plant produced more than 4 billion rounds of ammunition, and half of its employees were women.[60, 61] African-Americans and Native Americans also played a major role in working in factories in the Twin Cities. Other companies and industries in Minnesota also soon joined the fight; the St. Paul Ford

A propaganda poster recruited women ordinance workers, also known as WOWs

Plant transitioned to building armored cars and Honeywell built bombsights for bombers and other equipment for aircraft.[62] One of the biggest impacts came from Minnesota's Iron Range, which produced much of the iron ore for the U.S. war effort during World War II.

Believe It or Not

A group of 84 Minnesota Naval Reservists were part of the crew on the U.S.S. *Ward*, which fired the first U.S. shots against the Japanese in World War II.[63, 64] The ship was patrolling Pearl Harbor and encountered a Japanese midget submarine, which it sank with one of its guns. That gun is now located on the grounds of the Minnesota State Capitol.[65]

THE IRON RANGE AND THE WAR

Minnesota had a direct impact on the war; much of the equipment was made from materials from the Iron Range. If it was steel, there was a good chance that the iron came from Minnesota. Over the course of the war, Minnesota's Iron Range produced 269 million tons of iron ore. The heaviest U.S. battleship in the war, the famed U.S.S. *Iowa*, weighed somewhere in the ballpark of 45,000 tons.[66] It took about 3000 pounds of iron ore to make one ton of steel, so if we assume that the *Iowa* was all steel (it wasn't, but for the sake of this back-of-the-envelope calculation let's assume it was), that means the ore from Minnesota could have helped produce nearly 4,000 ships the size of the *Iowa*.[67]

Maritime Minnesota

Minnesota's iron ore industry directly led to its shipping industry. It might not seem like it, but the North Shore is a bit like Maine. There might not be lobsters or saltwater, but you'll find lighthouses, fishermen and huge ships on their way to the other Great Lakes, with some heading to the open ocean. Here's a brief look at Maritime Minnesota.

A World War II propaganda poster

Ports: It might seem strange, but thanks to the Great Lakes, Minnesota is a shipping destination. In fact, the twin ports of Duluth-Superior are the busiest ports on the Great Lakes, and together they are one of the busiest ports in the country. Duluth-Superior is regularly visited by a variety of ships, including massive 1000-foot ore boats and oceangoing vessels alike. Minnesota is a major destination thanks to our railroad connections and our plentiful resources; the primary cargoes leaving from Duluth are iron ore, coal, limestone and grain. Duluth-Superior isn't alone; several other Minnesota ports (including Two Harbors) are also quite busy, and the Mississippi River is also home to many boats, barges and other vessels.

Lighthouses: Minnesota's Lake Superior shore has eight lighthouses, and there are two privately run lighthouses on the Mississippi River. Several light-

1930s 1940s

houses on the North Shore, including the Two Harbors Lighthouse and Split Rock Lighthouse, are open for tours.

Wrecks: With ships come shipwrecks, and even though Minnesota's North Shore only encompasses a portion of Lake Superior, our shoreline is positively littered with wrecks, making scuba diving a popular pastime by the Big Lake. Some 550 shipwrecks (including the ill-fated *Edmund Fitzgerald*) are estimated to lie at the bottom of Lake Superior, with perhaps 50 in Minnesota waters. Sometimes, individual storms and wrecks led to major changes; the loss of the *Madeira* in 1905—a ship owned by a steel magnate—spurred the creation of Split Rock Lighthouse.

LINDY SUITS UP

Despite his very public fall from grace, once war was declared, Charles Lindbergh soon attempted to join the war effort. Once a colonel in the Air Corps, he had resigned his position in protest after President Roosevelt had publicly dubbed him a traitor.[68] He therefore attempted to find a way to support the effort, but was rebuffed at almost every turn. Eventually he served as a civilian consultant for United Aircraft, and though he wasn't a member of the armed services, he flew over 50 combat missions in the Pacific Theater and even shot down one enemy plane.[69, 70]

GERMAN PRISONERS OF WAR IN MINNESOTA AND A NOT-SO-GREAT ESCAPE

When prisoners were captured in Europe, they were often transferred to the U.S. Midwest, which was home to several camps for Axis prisoners of war. Minnesota housed a number of sub-camps of German prisoners. Some twenty camps were scattered across the state, with camps in places like Ada, Bena, Moorhead, Grand Rapids, Owatonna and Remer.[71] These prisoners performed manual labor—working in farm fields, making roads, and so on. While most of the prisoners had relatively fond memories of their time in Minnesota (some even emigrated after the war), a pair of Germans at the Bena camp—Heinz Schymalla and Walter Mai—attempted to escape and return to Germany. Unlike the famed Great Escape in Europe, their attempt was something of a bumbling affair: their end goal was to travel to Lake Winnibigoshish and the Mississippi River, then float to the Gulf of Mexico, where they hoped to find a neutral ship to travel to Germany and rejoin the fight. They used maps from a dictionary to plan their route, stashed away as much food as they could and obtained a change of clothing that lacked the conspicuous "PW" on the standard prisoner of war uniform.[72] They planned to sail on a flimsy raft that they'd hidden in the brush. (The vessel was one of several that the prisoners had been allowed to make to reach deeper water for swimming.)[73] Evading the guards, the pair managed to escape and reach the lake. They quickly ran into problems; the boat hardly floated and they had to wade through the cold water, nearly getting frostbite. Later on their voyage, they encountered a number of problems they hadn't anticipated; to reach the Mississippi River, they had to avoid a dam, and they also lacked the proper clothing for the cold November weather. If the escape attempt was half-baked, so was the search. Their absence wasn't discovered for some time, and while police (and the FBI) converged upon Bena, they neglected to notice the missing boat. In the end, the pair managed to stay on the run for five days, and they traveled 50 miles. Eventually, a chance encounter led an angler to call police, and they were quickly found and surrounded outside Grand Rapids.[74]

Believe It or Not

Ironically, there was also a German prisoner of war camp in New Ulm, which was founded by German immigrants. The site is now part of Flandrau State Park, and visitors can see (and stay at) the former camp, which is now part of the park's group camp area.

MINNESOTANS IN BATTLE

Minnesotans played a prominent role in the war. Minnesotan soldiers were present from the opening shots of the war at Pearl Harbor to the liberation of the concentrations camps at the end of the war in Europe.[75] In Europe, the 34th Infantry Division, which consisted mainly of soldiers from Minnesota and Iowa, was the first to land, and one of its members, a Private Henke of Hutchinson, was officially the first enlisted American soldier to enter Europe.[76] As it was the first to reach Europe, the 34th also saw more combat

**1930s
1940s**

days—a whopping 517—than any other division in the war. Minnesotans also fought bravely in the Pacific.[77]

All told, Minnesota contributed 1.93 percent of all the troops in the U.S. Army, and accounted for 2.11 percent of the dead and missing.[78] More than 6,430 Minnesotans died in the Army and Army Air Corps, and 1,474 died while serving in the other branches of the Armed Forces.[79] In all, some 7,900 Minnesotans died in the war. Every county in the state lost soldiers.

Believe It or Not

Fort Snelling was also home to a top-secret school that trained Japanese-American soldiers to serve as linguists and translators in the Pacific.[80]

A CHANGING CITYSCAPE AND A CHANGING MINNESOTA

When Minnesota's soldiers returned at the end of the war, Minnesota was a different place. The milling industry was all but dead—with most mills destroyed or abandoned by the 1950s. The mining industry was still producing vast amounts of iron—but soon it would begin a gradual decline. The population was growing, too. In 1940, Minnesota's population was 2.7 million. By the end of the baby boom, the state's population was 3.5 million. Many returning soldiers took advantage of the G.I. Bill or rejoined the work force, displacing the women and people of color who had worked in the factories during the war.

**1950s
1960s**

Believe It or Not

Not all of the mills are gone. The Pillsbury A-Mill is still standing; it ceased operations in 2003 and is now being converted into lofts for artists.

THE KOREAN WAR

Just five years after the end of World War II, Minnesotans would join the fight in Korea, which is often considered a forgotten war, overshadowed by the Second World War and the constant news reports from the later Vietnam War. Korea, though, was just as brutal as both wars. Minnesotans fought at the Battle of Chosin Reservoir where U.N. troops were outnumbered by 7 or 8 to 1.[81] By war's end in 1953, 725 Minnesotans had been killed in action in Korea.[82]

THE COLD WAR AND A BIG SCARE FOR WCCO LISTENERS

In a real respect, the Korean War and the later Vietnam War were battles in a much larger conflict: The Cold War. Even though Minnesota was nearly as far removed from the U.S.S.R. as one could get, signs of the Cold War were visible nearly everywhere. This was the era of *Duck and Cover* and Civil Defense. WCCO radio prepared (positively terrifying) automated messages to broadcast in the event of a nuclear war.[83] On one occasion in 1971, an "emergency action notification" was inadvertently triggered by a teletype error, and the wrong message—one warning of an impending attack—was sent to radio stations nationwide. Protocols dictated that regular programming stop and each station's announcer read out the alert. WCCO's announcer did just that on the air, and the result terrified listeners: "This station has interrupted its regular program at the request of the U.S. Government to participate in the Emergency Broadcast System."[84] Thankfully, it became clear almost immediately that it was an error.

A civil preparedness booklet from the U.S. Government

CIVIL RIGHTS IN MINNESOTA

The 1950s and the 1960s were an absolutely critical period for the Civil Rights movement, and a pair of Minnesotans—Roy Wilkins and Hubert Humphrey—played very important roles in the movement.[85] Born in

1950s
1960s

St. Louis, Wilkins led the NAACP from 1955 until 1977. His tenure coincided with some of the Civil Rights movements finest moments—from school integration in the South to the Voting Rights Act. Elected as Mayor of Minneapolis in 1945, Hubert Humphrey immediately set about to combat racism and inequality. [86] Later, in 1948 he helped make Civil Rights part of the Democratic Party's national platform, giving the movement a much needed boost.[87]

THE RONDO NEIGHBORHOOD

Despite this progress, structural racism was prevalent, as were the income, health and achievement gaps that persist to this day. The near-complete destruction of the Rondo Neighborhood during the construction of I-94 is a prime example of this. Located in St. Paul, the Rondo neighborhood was the oldest African-American neighborhood in the Twin Cities; when it came time to build I-94, the Rondo Neighborhood became collateral damage.[88] Residents protested, but they were soon forced to leave their homes, which were demolished. What remained of the neighborhood was

Civil Rights leader Roy Wilkins

bisected by the new highway, and the now-displaced residents found themselves amid an unfriendly and often predatory housing market.[89]

AN IMPORTANT ACCOUNT OF VIETNAM

One of the most famous accounts of Vietnam is by a Minnesotan. Tim O'Brien's book, *The Things They Carried*, is a book of short stories, but that doesn't make it untrue. On the contrary, its stories capture the horror and ambiguity of the war, as well as something of the complicated atmosphere stateside.

A Memorial

Not far from the Capitol Building, the Minnesota Vietnam Veterans Memorial honors the 68,000 Minnesotans who served in Vietnam, including the 1,120 Minnesotans who were killed in action or are listed as missing in action. [90]

MINNESOTA'S HMONG POPULATION

While we refer to it as the Vietnam War, the war spilled over into many neighboring nations, including Laos and Cambodia. In Laos, many members of the local Hmong population had been recruited to fight in what essentially became a civil war between Communists and anti-Communists.[91] When the Vietnam War ended, many Hmong were retaliated against, and tens of thousands were killed; many fled to the U.S., with thousands eventually settling in Minnesota.[92]

1960s present

Believe It or Not

The vast majority of Hmong Minnesotans are not immigrants; they are second- or third-generation citizens, yet they are often treated as newcomers.[93]

LIBERIANS AND SOMALIS IN MINNESOTA

In addition to Hmong immigrants, Minnesota is also home to many immigrants from Africa, including many from Liberia and Somalia. In many ways, last century's immigrants are a mirror image of more recent immigrants to Minnesota, and newer immigrants face the same types of prejudices that previous immigrants faced.

For proof, think of some of the unkind remarks you may have heard about these groups and compare them to this statement:

> We have great slum districts almost exclusively settled by the pauper outcasts . . . who drop even lower in the social scale here than the pits

1960s
present

into which they were born at home. They produce large and swarming hives of children, who grow up dirty, ignorant, depraved and utterly unfit for American citizenship. This is speaking, of course, in a general way. Everybody knows that some of these city-staying immigrants rise above their surroundings and make good citizens. But the tendency is the other way.

This appeared in Minnesota's *Princeton Union* on October 3, 1907, and the author was talking about the recent immigrants to the U.S., including the Irish, Germans, Swedes and Norwegians who now make up much of Minnesota's population.[94]

A MULTICULTURAL MENU

Minnesota's multicultural heritage isn't hard to find, thanks to the state's wide variety of culinary options. Here are a few popular dishes from a number of cultures in Minnesota.

Pasty (*past*-ee), a meat pie brought to Minnesota by miners from Cornwall in the U.K.

Porketta, a roasted pork dish from Italy

Potica, a sweet dessert from Slovenia

Potato sausage, from Sweden

Sarma, grape or cabbage leaves stuffed with meat, from Croatia

Fry bread, a deep-fried bread, from the Ojibwe culture

Blueberry wojapi, a thick pudding-like dish, from the Dakota culture

Knoephla soup, a German soup consisting of dumplings and chicken

Krumkake, a Norwegian waffle cookie

Phở, a Hmong noodle soup

FAMOUS NAMES AND PLACES IN MINNESOTA HISTORY, EXPLAINED

From Nicollet Avenue in Minneapolis to the south-central Minnesota city of Le Sueur, Minnesota's towns, streets and places are replete with famous names. Some of the names are obvious, but others are far less familiar. This is a brief rundown of just some of the more famous places in Minnesota. Given that there are many different places or structures named for some people (say, Father Hennepin), I've only listed one primary example for each.

Brule Lake (in the BWCAW) is named for Etienne Brule, who was a French explorer and likely the first European to see Lake Superior.

Bud Grant Way (Minneapolis) is named for Bud Grant, who coached the Minnesota Vikings for 18 seasons, leading them to four Super Bowl appearances.

Cleveland Avenue (Minneapolis)
is named for landscape architect Horace Cleveland, who created what would become the famous Grand Rounds in Minneapolis.

Crosby (city)
is named for George H. Crosby, a mining tycoon who founded Crosby and discovered iron ore on the Mesabi and the Cuyuna ranges.

Cuyuna (iron range)
is a combination of the names of Cuyler Adams, who discovered the Cuyuna range, and "Una," the name of his dog.

Duluth (city)
is named for Daniel Greysolon Sieur du Lhut, a French soldier and explorer who claimed all Dakota lands for France.

Faribault (city)
is named for Alexander Faribault, an American trader who founded the city that bears his name.

Fort Snelling (St. Paul) is named for Josiah Snelling, the fort's first commander.

Foshay Tower (Minneapolis)
is named for investor (and pyramid-scheme operator) Wilbur Foshay, who had the tower built.

Gustavus Adolphus College (St. Peter)
is named to honor Gustavus Adolphus, a king of Sweden from the seventeenth century; he was famous for turning Sweden into a world power.

Guthrie Theater (Minneapolis)
is named for Tyrone Guthrie, a theatrical director and the theater's founder.

Harmon Killebrew Drive (Bloomington)
is named for Harmon Killebrew, a Hall of Fame slugger and first baseman for the Minnesota Twins.

Hennepin Avenue (Minneapolis)
is named for Father Louis Hennepin, a French priest and missionary who explored the Midwest and is perhaps most famous for naming St. Anthony Falls.

Hermann the German Monument (New Ulm)
is dedicated to Arminius (also known as Hermann) a chieftain of a Germanic tribe that annihilated several Roman legions in 9 AD; Arminius was considered a national hero among many Germans (including German immigrants to Minnesota).

Hiawatha Avenue (Minneapolis)
is named for the title character of Henry Wadsworth Longfellow's epic poem, "The Song of Hiawatha."

James J. Hill House (St. Paul)
is named for James J. Hill, who built the Great Northern Railway.

Kirby Puckett Place (Minneapolis)
is named in honor of Kirby Puckett, a Hall of Fame center fielder for the Minnesota Twins.

Lake Calhoun (Minneapolis)
is named for the U.S. Secretary of War, John C. Calhoun, who ordered the U.S. Army to survey the land that would become Fort Snelling.

Lake Harriet (Minneapolis)
is named for Harriet Lovejoy, the wife of Colonel Henry Leavenworth, who founded Fort Snelling.

Lake Nokomis (Minneapolis)
is named for Nokomis, the grandmother of the hero Hiawatha in Henry Wadsworth Longfellow's "The Song of Hiawatha."

Le Sueur (city)
is named for Pierre-Charles Le Sueur, who was the first European to explore the Minnesota River Valley.

Loring Park (Minneapolis)
is named in honor of Charles Loring, a businessman and president of the Board of Park Commissioners; he was essential in developing the parks system.

Mariucci Arena (Minneapolis)
at the University of Minnesota is named in honor of John Mariucci, who was a standout hockey player for the Golden Gophers and later coached them.

Nicollet Mall (Minneapolis)
is named in honor of Joseph Nicollet, a French geographer who mapped the Upper Mississippi River Valley.

Northrop Auditorium (Minneapolis)
is located on the University of Minnesota campus and is named for Cyrus Northrop, the University's second president.

Ordway Center (St. Paul)
was named in honor of the Ordway family, especially Sally Ordway Irvine, a 3M heiress who sought to build the theater.

Pillsbury (company)
was founded by John S. Pillsbury and his nephew, Charles Alfred Pillsbury; John Pillsbury would later go on to become Minnesota's eighth governor.

Radisson Hotels
are named for French trader and explorer Pierre-Esprit Radisson, who traveled to Minnesota along with Médard des Groseilliers; they visited Minnesota in the 1650s and were likely the first Europeans to reach Minnesota.

Ramsey County
is named for Alexander Ramsey, the second governor of Minnesota and also a U.S. Senator.

Reverend Martin Luther King Jr. Boulevard (St. Paul)
is named for the legendary civil rights figure, and it runs in front of the State Capitol.

Rod Carew Drive (Minneapolis)
is named for Rod Carew, a Hall of Fame infielder and batter for the Minnesota Twins.

Roy Wilkins Auditorium (St. Paul)
is named in honor of civil rights leader Roy Wilkins, who was also a longtime leader of the NAACP.

Minnesota's Peoples and Places

Sartell (city)

is named for Joseph B. Sartell, a millwright and one of the first Europeans to live in the town of Sartell.

Shakopee (city)

is named for a Dakota chief who was a signatory to many important treaties and who served as a guide to Joseph Nicollet.

Sibley County

is named for Henry Hastings Sibley, the first governor of Minnesota, and also the commander of the state militia in the U.S.-Dakota War of 1862.

Theodore Wirth Park (Minneapolis)

is named in honor of Theodore Wirth, a parks superintendent who helped develop and plan the park system of Minneapolis.

Walker Art Center (Minneapolis)

is named for lumber tycoon Thomas Walker, founder of the Red River Lumber Company and an avid art collector; he founded the Walker by adding a room to his house and allowing visitors to view his private collection.

Washburn "A" Mill Ruins (Minneapolis)

are the remnants of the Washburn "A" Mill, the successor to the original "A" Mill, which was destroyed in a flour dust explosion. (The new Washburn Mill burned down in 1991, but it was later turned into a park and the Mill City Museum.) The Washburn mill is named for Cadwallader G. Washburn, who opened the Minneapolis Milling Company; he later founded the Washburn-Crosby company, which would eventually become General Mills.

Williams Arena (Minneapolis)

is the home of Golden Gophers Basketball, and is named for Dr. Henry L. Williams, the University's football coach during the first two decades of the twentieth century.

A LOOK AT MINNESOTA'S DEMOGRAPHICS

From our higher-than-average household income and impressive high school graduation rate to the state's sheer size, Minnesota's demographics may surprise you. The following data is culled from the 2010 Census. Where possible, more recent estimates are included.

POPULATION	MINNESOTA	USA
Population, 2013 estimate	5,420,380	316,128,839
Population, 2010	5,303,925	308,745,538
Persons under 5 years	6.4%	6.3%
Persons under 18 years	23.6%	23.3%
Persons 65 years and over	13.9%	14.1%
Female persons	50.3%	50.8%

ETHNIC BACKGROUND*	MINNESOTA	USA
White	81.9%	62.6%
Black or African American	5.7%	13.2%
American Indian and Alaska Native	1.3%	1.2%
Asian	4.5%	5.3%
Native Hawaiian and Other Pacific Islander	0.1%	0.2%
Two or More Races	2.3%	2.4%
Hispanic or Latino	5.0%	17.1%

*Because some of these totals were estimates by the Census Bureau in 2013 (and not finalized numbers from the 2010 census) these percentages total up to 100.8 percent.

EDUCATION, ANCESTRY AND VETERANS

	MINNESOTA	USA
Foreign born persons, 2009–2013	7.3%	12.9%
Persons speaking language other than English at home, five and older, 2009–2013	10.7%	20.7%
High school graduate or higher, percent of persons twenty-five and older, 2009–2013	92.1%	86.0%
Bachelor's degree or higher, percent of persons twenty-five and older, 2009–2013	32.6%	28.8%
Veterans, 2009–2013	366,990	21,263,779

INCOME

	MINNESOTA	USA
Median household income, 2009–2013	$59,836	$53,046
Persons below poverty level, 2009–2013	11.5%	15.4%

GEOGRAPHY

	MINNESOTA	USA
Land area in square miles	79,626.74**	3,531,905.43
Persons per square mile, 2010	66.6	87.4
Shoreline***	183,000 miles	95,000 miles

**For comparison, this is only slightly smaller than the entirety of Ireland.

*** Minnesota's shoreline total is via www.chrisfinke.com and includes lakes, streams and rivers; the USA total is via noaa.gov and is for ocean coastline only. It's a bit apples-to-oranges, but it still gives you a rough idea of just how much shoreline we have.

MINNESOTA'S POPULATION, FROM THE TERRITORIAL ERA ON

YEAR	POPULATION	YEAR	POPULATION
1850	6,077	1940	2,792,300
1860	172,023	1950	2,982,483
1870	439,706	1960	3,413,864
1880	780,773	1970	3,804,971
1890	1,310,283	1980	4,075,970
1900	1,751,394	1990	4,375,099
1910	2,075,708	2000	4,919,479
1920	2,387,125	2010	5,303,925
1930	2,563,953		

Data from U.S. Census Bureau (www.census.gov)

FOREIGN-BORN POPULATION OF MINNEAPOLIS, OVER TIME

The numbers don't lie: Minnesota's population has always consisted of a significant number of newcomers. As an example, check out just how much of Minneapolis' population has consisted of foreign-born folks over the years.

YEAR	POPULATION	YEAR	POPULATION
1880	32%	1950	9.4%
1890	36.8%	1960	7.1%
1900	30.1%	1970	4.8%
1910	28.6%	1980	4.9%
1920	23.2%	1990	6.1%
1930	17.5%	2000	14.5%
1940	13.1%	2009–2013	15.9%

All data from the U.S. Census Bureau (www.census.gov); 2009–2013 data from the U.S. Census American Community Survey.

WHERE DID MINNESOTANS ORIGINATE?

When it comes to the question of where Minnesotans came from—our ancestry—the simple answer is: almost everywhere. The following list is a selection of just a few of the countries where Minnesotans trace their roots.

ANCESTRY	POPULATION IN 2013	ANCESTRY	POPULATION IN 2013
American Indian	101,900	Norwegian	561,501
Asian	243,917	Polish	148,813
Czech	49,892	Russian	27,514
Danish	39,118	Scandinavian	59,253
Dutch	53,744	Scotch-Irish	18,147
English	170,543	Scottish	34,973
Finnish	69,399	Ethiopian	15,163
French (except Basque)	94,825	Liberian	7,348
French Canadian	32,965	Nigerian	6,112
German	1,403,783	Somali	35,872
Irish	308,624	Swedish	263,372
Hispanic/Latino	271,019	Ukrainian	11,548
Italian	86,346		

Note: This list is largely culled from the U.S. Census Bureau's 2009–2013 American Community Survey. The American Indian, Asian and Hispanic/Latino population totals are from U.S. Census "Fast Facts" for Minnesota (http://factfinder.census.gov). Also, keep in mind that residents often claim more than one ancestry; this list is by no means definitive.

Resources

FROM PREHISTORY TO SETTLEMENT

1. Curry, Andrew. Ancient migration: Coming to America. May 3, 2012. www.nature.com/news/ancient-migration-coming-to-america-1.10-562

2. Gibbon, Guy. *Archaeology of Minnesota: The Prehistory of the Upper Mississippi River Region*. Minneapolis, Minnesota: University of Minnesota Press, 2012.

3. Chun Li, et al. An ancestral turtle from the Late Triassic of southwestern China. November 27, 2008. www.nature.com/nature/journal/v456/n7221/full/nature07533.html

4. Pringle, Heather. "The 1st Americans." *Scientific American*, 2011: 36–45.

5. *Ibid*.

6. Nelson J.R. Fagundes, et al. "Mitochondrial Population Genomics Supports a Single Pre-Clovis Origin with a Coastal Route for the Peopling of the Americas." *American Journal of Human Genetics*, March 2008.

7. Ferentinos, George. "Early seafaring activity in the southern Ionian Islands, Mediterranean Sea." *Journal of Archaeological Science* 39, no. 7, July 2012.

8. *Ibid*.

9. Sriram Sankararaman, et al. "The genomic landscape of Neanderthal ancestry in present-day humans." *Nature*. Volume 507, March 2014.

10. Gibbon, Guy. *Archaeology of Minnesota: The Prehistory of the Upper Mississippi River Region*. Minneapolis, Minnesota: University of Minnesota Press, 2012.

11. *Ibid*.

12. *Ibid*.

13. *Ibid*.

14. *Ibid*.

15. Smetan, Mary Jane. "Indian Burial Grounds, Rest in Peace." *StarTribune*. July 22, 2009. www.startribune.com/local/south/51103647.html

16. Nelson, Paul. St. Paul's Indian Burial Mounds. May 20, 2008. http://digitalcommons.macalester.edu/cgi/viewcontent.cgi?article=1000&context=igcstaffpub

17. Tekiela, Stan. *Trees of Minnesota*. Cambridge: Adventure Publications, 2002.

18. USDA Natural Resource Conservation Service. Plants Profile for *Pinus strobus* (eastern white pine). http://plants.usda.gov/core/profile?symbol=pist

19. Welby Smith and Jan Shaw Wolff. "Wildly Adaptable Trees." *Minnesota Conservation Volunteer,* September–October 2008.

20. The State of Minnesota. "Wetlands Restoration Strategy." Minnesota Board of Water and Soil Resources. January 2009. www.bwsr.state.mn.us/wetlands/Restoration_Strategy.pdf

21. Minnesota Department of Natural Resources. "Prairie grasslands description." www.dnr.state.mn.us/snas/prairie_description.html

22. Daniels, John D. "The Indian Population of North America in 1492." *The William and Mary Quarterly* 49, no. 2 (April 1992).

23. Watkins, Thayer. *The History of the Aztecs.* www.sjsu.edu/faculty/watkins/aztecs.htm

24. Smithsonian Institute. "Lakota Winter Counts." http://wintercounts.si.edu/html_version/html/socialstructure.html

25. *Ibid.*

26. Minnesota Historical Society. Oceti Šakowiŋ - The Seven Council Fires. http://collections.mnhs.org/sevencouncilfires/

27. *Encyclopedia Britannica.* Sioux. August 16, 2014. www.britannica.com/EBchecked/topic/546408/Sioux/284093/The-Sioux-way-of-life

28. Ojibwe.org. "About the Anishinaabe-Ojibwe." www.ojibwe.org/home/about_anish.html

29. Northern Michigan University. "Recorded in Stone: Voices on the Marquette Iron Range." http://voices.nmu.edu/content.asp?PageName=Index

30. Eid, Leroy. "The Ojibwa-Iroquois War: One War the Five Nations Didn't Win." *Ethnohistory.* Vol. 26, No. 4, Autumn, 1979.

31. Fitzpatrick-Matthews, Keith. "The Kensington Runestone." www.badarchaeology.com/?page_id=1311

32. McCormick, Douglas. "Columbus's Geographical Miscalculations." October 9, 2012. http://spectrum.ieee.org/tech-talk/at-work/test-and-measurement/columbuss-geographical-miscalculations

33. Nunn, Nathan, and Nancy Qian. "The Columbian Exchange: A History of Disease, Food, and Ideas." *Journal of Economic Perspectives* 24, No. 2, 2010.

34. *Ibid.*

35. Holand, Hjalmar. "Radisson's Two Western Journeys." *Minnesota History,* June 1934.

36. Hudson's Bay Company. "HBC Timeline." www.hbcheritage.ca/content/timeline

37. —. "Our History: People: Explorers: Radisson and des Groseilliers." www.hbcheritage.ca/hbcheritage/history/people/explorers/radisson.asp

38. Kellogg, Louise Phillips. "The French Regime in the Great Lakes Country." *Minnesota History Magazine*. December 1931. http://collections.mnhs.org/MNHistoryMagazine/articles/12/v12i04p347-358.pdf

39. Schmirler, A.A.A. "Wisconsin's Lost Missionary: The Mystery of Father Rene Menard." *The Wisconsin Magazine of History*, Winter 1961–1962.

40. Wisconsin State Historical Society. "Odd Wisconsin: First priest to reach state disappeared during canoe trip." *Wisconsin State Journal*. December 4, 2014. http://host.madison.com/news/local/odd-wisconsin-first-priest-to-reach-state-disappeared-during-canoe/article_ff01c76a-3e19-11e2-93ff-001a4bcf887a.html#ixzz3E9rrYLzS

41. Neill, Edward D. "The history of Minnesota; from the earliest French explorations to the present time..." Making of America Books, University of Michigan Library. http://quod.lib.umich.edu/m/moa/aja3456.0001.001/109?page=root;size=100;view=image

42. Kellogg, Louise Phillips. "The French Regime in the Great Lakes Country." *Minnesota History Magazine*. December 1931. http://collections.mnhs.org/MNHistoryMagazine/articles/12/v12i04p347-358.pdf

43. *Ibid*.

44. Westerman, Gwen, and Bruce White. *Mni Sota Makoce: The Land of the Dakota*. St. Paul, MN: Minnesota Historical Society Press.

45. *Ibid*.

46. Kellogg, Louise Phillips. "The French Regime in the Great Lakes Country." *Minnesota History Magazine*. December 1931. http://collections.mnhs.org/MNHistoryMagazine/articles/12/v12i04p347-358.pdf

47. Blegen, Theodore. *Minnesota: A History of the State.* Minneapolis, MN: University Of Minnesota Press, 1975.

48. *Ibid*.

49. *Ibid*.

50. Merriam-Webster. "Coureur de bois." www.merriam-webster.com/dictionary/coureur de bois

51. Parks Canada. "The Fur Trade at Lachine National Historic Site." www.pc.gc.ca/eng/lhn-nhs/qc/lachine/visit/faq.aspx

52. Minnesota Humanities Center. "The Voyageurs." www.mnhum.org/Resources/The Voyageurs.pdf

53. Hillman, Mike. "La Bonga: The Greatest Voyageur," *Boundary Waters Journa*l. Summer 2010.

54. Hennepin, Louis. *A Description of Louisiana*. Edited by John Gillmary Shea. New York, J.G. Shea, 1880. Accessed via InternetArchive.org, https://archive.org/details/descriptionoflou00henn

55. U.S. Army Corps of Engineers. "Engineering the Falls: The Corps Role at St. Anthony Falls." St. Paul District, Army Corps of Engineers. www.mvp.usace.army.mil/Portals/57/docs/Home/History/engineering.pdf

56. Minnesota Historical Society. "Timeline: St. Anthony Falls." www.mnhs.org/school/online/communities/timelines/timelines_st_anthony.php

57. The Library of Congress. "Louisiana Purchase." www.loc.gov/rr/program/bib/ourdocs/Louisiana.html

58. Carver, Jonathan. *"Travels through the interior parts of North America, in the years 1766, 1767, and 1768 (1781)."* Accessed via InternetArchive.org. https://archive.org/details/travelsthroughin00carv

59. Falch, Sara. "(Thesis) Jonathan Carver's Footprints: The Carver Land Grant Case of 1825 and the Impact of American Indian Policy." Minds@UW. June 25, 2008. https://minds.wisconsin.edu/handle/1793/2868

60. Gould, Heidi. "Jonathan Carver: explorer, mapmaker, author and subject of controversy." January 1, 2014. www.minnpost.com/mnopedia/2014/01/jonathan-carver-explorer-mapmaker-author-and-subject-controversy

61. Jacobson, Ryan. *Ghostly Tales of Minnesota*. Cambridge, MN: Adventure Publications, 2009.

62. *Ibid.*

63. The North West Company. "History." www.northwest.ca/about-us/history.php#prettyPhoto[history]/12/

64. Risjord, Norman K. *A Popular History of Minnesota*. St. Paul, MN: Minnesota Historical Society Press, 2005.

65. Woolworth, Nancy. "Grand Portage in the Revolutionary War." *Minnesota History Magazine*. Summer 1975. 1. http://collections.mnhs.org/MNHistoryMagazine/articles/44/v44i06p198-208.pdf

66. *Ibid.*

67. U.S. State Department, Office of the Historian. "Milestones: 1784–1800; John Jay's Treaty, 1794–95." https://history.state.gov/milestones/1784-1800/jay-treaty

68. Minnesota Historical Society. "U.S.-Dakota War: Minnesota Treaty Interactive." http://usdakotawar.org/history/treaties/minnesota-treaty-interactive

69. *Ibid.*

70. *Ibid.*

71. Minnesota Historical Society. "U.S.-Dakota War: Bdote." www.usdakotawar.org/history/dakota-homeland-land-lifestyle/bdote

72. *Ibid.*

73. French, Warren. "Burr, Aaron," *Handbook of Texas Online.* Published by the Texas State Historical Association. www.tshaonline.org/handbook/online/articles/fbu57

74. Minnesota Historical Society. "Historic Fort Snelling, Timeline." www.historicfortsnelling.org/history/timeline

75. Minnesota Historical Society. "U.S.-Dakota War: Minnesota Treaty Interactive." http://usdakotawar.org/history/treaties/minnesota-treaty-interactive

76. *Ibid*.

77. Johnson, Deane. *The Best of Itasca: A Guide to Minnesota's Oldest State Park*. Cambridge, Minnesota: Adventure Publications, 2014.

78. *Ibid*.

79. *Ibid*.

80. Minnesota Historical Society. "U.S.-Dakota War: Minnesota Treaty Interactive." http://usdakotawar.org/history/treaties/minnesota-treaty-interactive

81. *Ibid*.

82. *Ibid*.

83. United States National Park Service. "Fountain Cave." National Parks Service. www.nps.gov/miss/planyourvisit/founcave.htm

84. Minnesota Legal History Project. "The Organic Act." www.minnesotalegalhistoryproject.org/assets/Microsoft Word - Organic Act.pdf

85. Ho-Chunk Nation. "About | Ho-Chunk Nation." www.ho-chunknation.com/about.aspx

86. Minnesota Military Museum. "Forts on the Minnesota Frontier." www.mnmilitarymuseum.org/files/7713/2249/9100/Forts_on_the_Minnesota_Frontier.pdf

87. Qualey, Carlton. "Pioneer Norwegian Settlement in Minnesota." *Minnesota History Magazine*, September 1, 1931. http://collections.mnhs.org/MNHistoryMagazine/articles/12/v12i03p247-280.pdf

88. City of Saint Paul, MN. "History, Overview." www.stpaul.gov/index.aspx?NID=1013

89. Hennepin County Library - A History of Minneapolis. "A History of Minneapolis." www.hclib.org/pub/search/specialcollections/mplshistory/?id=4

90. *Ibid*.

91. *Ibid*.

92. *Ibid*.

93. Risjord, Norman K. *A Popular History of Minnesota*. St. Paul, MN: Minnesota Historical Society Press, 2005.

94. Bright, William. *Native American Placenames of the United States*. Norman: University of Oklahoma Press, 2004.

95. Schaetzl, Randall. GEO 333, Geography of Michigan. "Place Names." Michigan State University, http://web2.geo.msu.edu/geogmich/placenames.html

96. Coombe, Rosemary J. "Embodied Trademarks: Mimemis and Alterity on American Commercial Frontiers." *Cultural Anthropology: Journal of the Society for Cultural Anthropology*, Issue 11, No. 2, 1996. www.academia.edu/755084/_Embodied_Trademarks_Mimesis_and_Alterity_On_American_Commercial_Frontiers_

FROM SAWDUST CITY TO FLOUR POWER

1. U.S. Census Office. "Dates of Statehood for 50 U.S. States." www.1930census.com/united_states_50_states_by_statehood.php

2. Risjord, Norman K. *A Popular History of Minnesota*. St. Paul, MN: Minnesota Historical Society Press, 2005.

3. Historic Fort Snelling. "Slavery at Fort Snelling (1820s–1850s)." www.historicfortsnelling.org/history/slavery-fort-snelling

4. *Ibid*.

5. Justia U.S. Supreme Court Center. "Scott v. Sandford, 60 U.S. 393." https://supreme.justia.com/cases/federal/us/60/393/case.html

6. Missouri State Archives. "Missouri's Dred Scott Case, 1846–1857." Missouri Digital Heritage: Collections: Dred Scott Case, 1846–1857. www.sos.mo.gov/archives/resources/africanamerican/scott/scott.asp

7. Espinoza, Ambar. "St. Cloud Professor Unearths History of Slavery in Minnesota." Minnesota Public Radio News. www.mprnews.org/story/2010/05/07/upper-mississippi-slavery

8. *Minnesota in the Civil and Indian Wars*, 1861–1865. St. Paul, Minn.: *Pioneer Press*, 1890. Accessed via Google Books, http://books.google.com/books/about/Minnesota_in_the_Civil_and_Indian_Wars_1.html?id=ZuoLAAAAIAAJ

9. U.S. Census Bureau. "Resident Population and Apportionment of the U.S. House of Representatives." www.census.gov/dmd/www/resapport/states/minnesota.pdf

10. Frank, Lisa Tendrich. *Women in the American Civil War*. Santa Barbara, Calif.: ABC-CLIO, 2008.

11. United States National Park Service. "Battle Summary: Manassas, First, VA." National Parks Service. Accessed September 23, 2014. www.nps.gov/hps/abpp/battles/va005.htm

12. Albin, Maurice. "In Praise of Anesthesia: Two Case Studies of Pain and Suffering during Major Surgical Procedures with and without Anesthesia in the United States Civil War-1861–65." *Scandinavian Journal of Pain*, Volume 4, no. Issue 4, 243–46.

13. Sons of Union Veterans of the Civil War. "SUVCW—Honorary Commander-in-Chief Albert Woolson." http://suvcw.org/pcinc/woolson.htm

14. Minnesota Historical Society. "The U.S.-Dakota War: Broken Promises." www.usdakotawar.org/history/treaties/broken-promises

15. Minnesota Historical Society. "The U.S.-Dakota War: Andrew Myrick." www.usdakotawar.org/history/andrew-myrick

16. Minnesota Historical Society. "Taoyateduta Is Not a Coward (speech)." *Minnesota History Magazine,* September, 1962.

17. U.S. Census Bureau. "Resident Population and Apportionment of the U.S. House of Representatives." www.census.gov/dmd/www/resapport/states/minnesota.pdf

18. Minnesota Historical Society. "Historic Sites: Lower Sioux Agency, History." http://sites.mnhs.org/historic-sites/lower-sioux-agency/history

19. Linder, Douglas. "The Dakota Conflict (Sioux Uprising) Trials of 1862." Famous American Trials. http://law2.umkc.edu/faculty/projects/ftrials/dakota/Dak_account.html

20. Civil War Sites Advisory Commission Report. "Battle Summaries: Fort Ridgely." www.cr.nps.gov/hps/abpp/battles/mn001.htm

21. Minnesota Historical Society. "The U.S.-Dakota War: A Map of the U.S.-Dakota War." www.usdakotawar.org/history/war

22. *Minnesota in the Civil and Indian Wars, 1861–1865.* St. Paul, Minn.: *Pioneer Press*, 1890.

23. Murray County, Minnesota. "Slaughter Slough Wildlife Production Area." Murray County, Minnesota.

24. Minnesota Historical Society. "The Attacks on New Ulm." The U.S.-Dakota War of 1862. http://usdakotawar.org/history/attacks-new-ulm

25. Minnesota Historical Society. "Historic Sites: Birch Coulee Battlefield." http://sites.mnhs.org/historic-sites/birch-coulee-battlefield

26. Minnesota Historical Society. "The U.S.-Dakota War: War." www.usdakotawar.org/history/war

27. Wood Lake Battlefield Preservation Association. "Wood Lake Battlefield." www.woodlakebattlefield.com/battle-history.php

28. *Ibid.*

29. *Ibid.*

30. Minnesota Historical Society. "The U.S.-Dakota War: Aftermath." http://usdakotawar.org/history/aftermath

31. University of Pittsburgh Law Department. "Dakota." Famous Trials. http://jurist.law.pitt.edu/famoustrials/dakota.php

32. Minnesota Historical Society. "The U.S.-Dakota War: Forced Marches & Imprisonment." http://usdakotawar.org/history/aftermath/forced-marches-imprisonment

33. Brown, Curt. "In Little Crow's Wake, Horrors for the Dakota." *StarTribune*, August 12, 2012, Local section. www.startribune.com/local/166163736.html

34. Records of the Central Superintendency of Indian Affairs, 1813–1878. "1863." Washington: National Archives and Records Service, 1972. http://images.library.wisc.edu/History/EFacs/CommRep/AnnRep63/reference/history.annrep 63.i0012.pdf

35. Minnesota Historical Society. "The U.S.-Dakota War: Bounties." www.usdakotawar.org/history/aftermath/bounties

36. Winona County Historical Society. "Five Historians Describe the First Minnesota Regiment at Gettysburg." A Civil War Journal. www2.smumn.edu/deptpages/~history/civil_war/the.htm

37. *Ibid.*

38. Brown, Curt. "Sgt. Buckman's diary: The 150-year-old story of Gettysburg and the First Minnesota." *StarTribune*, June 30, 2013, Local sec. www.startribune.com/local/212817551.html

39. Winona County Historical Society. "Five Historians Describe the First Minnesota Regiment at Gettysburg." A Civil War Journal. www2.smumn.edu/deptpages/~history/civil_war/the.htm

40. Nelson, Tim. "No, Virginia, There Will Be No Battle Flag for the Gettysburg Anniversary." Minnesota Public Radio. June 25, 2013. http://blogs.mprnews.org/statewide/2013/06/no-virginia-there-will-be-no-battle-flag-for-the-gettysburg-anniversary/

41. National Archives and Records Administration, Teaching With Documents. "The Homestead Act of 1862." www.archives.gov/education/lessons/homestead-act/

42. Library of Congress. "*The Empire State of the Northwest* (book)." American Memory: Pioneering the Upper Midwest. Accessed via http://memory.loc.gov/

43. National Archives and Records Administration, Teaching With Documents. "The Homestead Act of 1862." www.archives.gov/education/lessons/homestead-act/

44. Great Northern Railway Historical Society. "What Was the Great Northern Railway?" Great Northern History. www.gnrhs.org/gn_history.htm

45. Cheyney, Edward G., and O. R. Levin. *Forestry in Minnesota*. St. Paul: Commissioner of Forestry and Fire Prevention, Cooperating with the Division of Forestry, University of Minnesota, 1929. http://files.dnr.state.mn.us/forestry/anniversary/documents/forestryInMinnesota-1929.pdf

46. Larson, Agnes M., and Bradley J. Gills. *White Pine Industry in Minnesota, a History*. Minneapolis: University of Minnesota Press, 2007.

47. USDA Forest Service. "Optional Laboratory: Calculating Board Footage In A Tree." Urban Forestry Lab. www.na.fs.fed.us/spfo/pubs/uf/lab_exercises/calc_board_footage.htm

48. Ellingson, Bob. "The General MacArthur White Pine." Every Root An Anchor: Wisconsin's Famous and Historic Trees. http://dnr.wi.gov/topic/ForestManagement/EveryRootAnAnchor/documents/072-GenMacArthurWhitePine.pdf

49. Arboristsite.com (forum)."Largest White Pine Ever Cut in Wisconsin?" www.arboristsite.com/community/threads/largest-white-pine-ever-cut-in-wisconsin.114292/

50. Burns, Russell, and Barbara Honkala. "Eastern White Pine." *Silvics Manual Volume 1.* www.na.fs.fed.us/pubs/silvics_manual/Volume_1/pinus/strobus.htm

51. Rocky Mountain Tree-Ring Research. "Oldlist." Rocky Mountain Tree-Ring Research, OLDLIST. www.rmtrr.org/oldlist.htm

52. Municipal Building Commission. "Fun Building Facts." www.municipalbuildingcommission.org/Fun_Facts.html

53. "Log Rafts on the Mississippi." *The Steamboat Times.* http://steamboattimes.com/rafts.html

54. Minnesota Historical Society. "Forests Then." Forest History Center. http://sites.mnhs.org/historic-sites/forest-history-center/forests-then

55. The Walker Art Museum. "Mission & History — About." Walker Art Center. www.walkerart.org/about/mission-history

56. Bachmann, Elizabeth. *A History of Forestry in Minnesota: With Particular Reference to Forestry Legislation.* St. Paul, Minn.: Association of Minnesota Division of Lands and Forestry Employees, 1969. Accessed via Minnesota DNR website. http://files.dnr.state.mn.us/forestry/anniversary/documents/historyofForestry-1969.pdf

57. Fins, Lauren, and Wildlife Forest. *Return of the Giants: Restoring White Pine Ecosystems by Breeding and Aggressive Planting of Blister Rust-resistant White Pines.* Moscow, ID: University of Idaho, 2001. Accessed via the Forest Service website, www.fs.fed.us/rm/pubs_other/rmrs_2001_fins_l001.pdf

58. Pennefeather, Shannon M. *Mill City: A Visual History of the Minneapolis Mill District.* St. Paul, MN: Minnesota Historical Society Press, 2003.

59. Fuller, John. "How Waterfalls Work." HowStuffWorks. http://geography.howstuffworks.com/terms-and-associations/waterfall1.htm

60. National Center for Earth-surface Dynamics. "The Eastman Tunnel Collapse: A Case Study of Human Impact on Nature." A History of Saint Anthony Falls. Accessed September 24, 2014. www.esci.umn.edu/courses/1001/1001_kirkby/SAFL/WEBSITEPAGES/5.htm

61. *Ibid.*

62. U.S. Army Corps of Engineers. "Engineering at the Falls: The Corps Role at St. Anthony Falls." U.S. Army Corps of Engineers. www.mvp.usace.army.mil/Portals/57/docs/Home/History/engineering.pdf

63. *Ibid.*

64. *Ibid.*

65. *Ibid.*

66. Blegen, Theodore. *Minnesota: A History of the State.* Minneapolis, MN: University Of Minnesota Press, 1975.

67. National Park Service. "Little American Island." Voyageurs National Park. www.nps.gov/voya/historyculture/upload/Little-American-Brochure-pubin-brown-web-quality.pdf

68. Minnesota Department of Natural Resources. "Minnesota Mining History." Digging into MN Minerals: Minnesota DNR. www.dnr.state.mn.us/education/geology/digging/history.html

69. Iron Range Resources and Rehabilitation Board. "History of the Iron Range." Data Center. http://mn.gov/irrrb/DataCenter/history/history-iron-range.jsp

70. Sirijimaki, John. "The People of the Iron Range." *Minnesota History Magazine*, June 1, 1946. http://collections.mnhs.org/MNHistoryMagazine/articles/48/v48i03p094-107.pdf

71. Iron Range Resources and Rehabilitation Board. "History of the Iron Range." Data Center. http://mn.gov/irrrb/DataCenter/history/history-iron-range.jsp

72. Sirijimaki, John. "The People of the Iron Range." *Minnesota History Magazine*, June 1, 1946. http://collections.mnhs.org/MNHistoryMagazine/articles/48/v48i03p094-107.pdf

73. Combs, Marianne. "Minnesota Architecture: Hibbing High School." State of the Arts (blog), Minnesota Public Radio. http://blogs.mprnews.org/state-of-the-arts/2011/07/minnesota-architecture-hibbing-high-school/

74. Jacobson, Ryan. *Minnesota Hauntings: Ghost Stories from the Land of 10,000 Lakes.* Cambridge: Adventure Publications, 2010.

75. Hise, Charles Richard. *The Iron-ore Deposits of the Lake Superior Region.* Washington, D.C.: U.S. Govt. Print. Office, 1901. Accessed via Google Books, books.google.com/books?id=TmrhAAAAMAAJ

76. Minnesota-Mines, Mining Artifacts and History. "Minnesota-Mines." www.miningartifacts.org/minnesota-mines.html

77. Appleby, William Remsen, and Edmund Newton. *Preliminary Concentration Tests on Cuyuna Ores.* Minneapolis: University of Minnesota, 1915. Accessed via Google Books, books.google.com/books?id=n-89AQAAMAAJ

FROM WORLD WAR I TO THE PRESENT DAY

1. First World War.com. "Primary Documents - U.S. Espionage Act, 15 June 1917." www.firstworldwar.com/source/espionageact.htm

2. McMurry, Martha. "Turn of the Century: Minnesota's Population in 1900 and Today." St. Paul, MN: Minnesota Planning, State Demographic Center, 1999.

Resources

3. Burnquist, J. A. A. Report of Minnesota Commission of Public Safety. St. Paul: [L.F. Dow], 1919. Accessed via Internetarchive.org, http://archive.org/stream/reportofminnesot00minnrich/reportofminnesot00minnrich_djvu.txt

4. *Ibid.*

5. "Fair Play Found in Times of War." *New Ulm Review*, July 17, 1917. Library of Congress. Chronicling America Digital Newspaper Archive. http://chroniclingamerica.loc.gov/lccn/sn89081128/1917-07-18/ed-1/seq-1/

6. Rippley, La Vern. "Conflict in the Classroom: Anti-Germanism in Minnesota Schools, 1917–1919." *Minnesota History Magazine*, March 1, 1981, http://collections.mnhs.org/MNHistoryMagazine/articles/47/v47i05p170-183.pdf

7. Risjord, Norman K. *A Popular History of Minnesota*. St. Paul, MN: Minnesota Historical Society Press, 2005.

8. Haulsee, W. M. *Soldiers of the Great War*. Washington, D.C.: Soldiers Record Pub. Association, 1920. Accessed via Google Books, http://books.google.com/books?id=vcwMAAAAYAAJ&printsec=frontcover&source=gbs_ge_summary_r&cad=0

9. League of Women Voters Minnesota. "Important Dates in League History." www.lwvmn.org/page.aspx?pid=600

10. *The 88th Division in the World War of 1914–1918*. New York: Wynkoop Hallenbeck Crawford Company, 1919. Accessed via Internetarchive.org, https://archive.org/details/thdivisioninwor00unkngoog

11. Stuhler, Barbara. "Organizing for the Vote: Leader's of Minnesota's Woman Suffrage Movement." *Minnesota History Magazine*, September 1, 1995. http://collections.mnhs.org/MNHistoryMagazine/articles/54/v54i07p290-303.pdf

12. League of Women Voters, Duluth. "Important Dates in League History." www.lwvduluth.org/important-dates-in-league-history.html

13. Hanson, David. "The Eighteenth Amendment." *Alcohol: Problems and Solutions*; State University of New York, Potsdam.

14. Hanson, David. "Wayne Wheeler." *Alcohol: Problems and Solutions*; State University of New York, Potsdam.

15. U.S. Joint Chiefs of Staff. "Estimate of the Situation Red and Tentative Joint Basic Plan Red." Strategytheory.org. May 1, 1930. http://strategytheory.org/military/us/joint_board/Estimate of the Situation - Red and Tentative Joint Basic Plan - Red.pdf

16. TaoYue.com. "A Plan for a Preemptive Strike on the United States by the British Dominion of Canada, circa 1921." www.taoyue.com/stacks/articles/defence-scheme-one.html

17. Minnesota Department of Transportation. "Aviation Firsts - First Balloon Ascent in Minnesota." www.dot.state.mn.us/aero/aviationeducation/museum/aviation_firsts/minnesota.html

18. Bach Dunn, Marianne. "Zeppelin in Minnesota: The Count's Own Story." *Minnesota History Magazine*, June 1, 1967. http://collections.mnhs.org/MNHistoryMagazine/articles/40/v40i06p265-278.pdf

19. *Ibid.*

20. Sandvick, Gerald. "The Birth of Powered Flight in Minnesota." *Minnesota History Magazine*, June 1, 1982. http://collections.mnhs.org/MNHistoryMagazine/articles/48/v48i02p046-059.pdf

21. United States National Park Service. "1903, The First Flight." National Parks Service, Wright Brothers National Memorial. September 5, 2014. www.nps.gov/wrbr/historyculture/thefirstflight.htm

22. The Early Birds of Aviation. "Rosto in Norway." www.rcooper.0catch.com/erosto1.htm

23. Minnesota Department of Transportation. "Aviation Firsts - First Air Show in Minnesota." www.dot.state.mn.us/aero/aviationeducation/museum/aviation_firsts/minnesota.html

24. Doherty, Trafford. "Glenn H. Curtiss - 100 Years Ago." Glenn H. Curtiss Museum. www.glennhcurtissmuseum.org/educational/glenn_curtiss.html

25. *Ibid*.

26. Hoffbeck, Steven. "Shooting Star: Aviator Jimmie Ward of Crookston." *Minnesota History Magazine*, December 1, 1995. http://collections.mnhs.org/MNHistoryMagazine/articles/54/v54i08p330-341.pdf

27. *Ibid*.

28. The Page of the Parks Airport Register. "Charles W. "Speed" Holman." www.parksfield.org/people/holman_cw/

29. United States Postal Service. "Airmail." https://about.usps.com/who-we-are/postal-history/airmail.pdf. https://about.usps.com/who-we-are/postal-history/airmail.pdf

30. Sandvick, Gerald. "Enterprise in the Skies." *Minnesota History Magazine*, September 1, 1986. http://collections.mnhs.org/MNHistoryMagazine/articles/50/v50i03p086-098.pdf

31. Aero News Network. "The Secret Of The White Bird." www.aero-news.net/index.cfm?do=main.textpost&id=c22b14fc-5c71-4b9b-ac77-a08f5528439f

32. Public Broadcasting System. "Lindbergh: Lindbergh's Transatlantic Flight: New York to Paris." www.pbs.org/wgbh/amex/lindbergh/maps/flighttext.html

33. History.com. "May 21, 1927, Lindbergh Lands in Paris." www.history.com/this-day-in-history/lindbergh-lands-in-paris

34. Public Broadcasting System. "Lindbergh: Lindbergh's Transatlantic Flight: New York to Paris." www.pbs.org/wgbh/amex/lindbergh/maps/flighttext.html

35. "Lindbergh Does It! May 21, 1927." On This Day, *New York Times*. www.nytimes.com/learning/general/onthisday/big/0521.html

36. Wilkinson, Stephan. "The Legendary Lockheed Constellation." History Net Where History Comes Alive World US History Online The Legendary Lockheed Constellation Comments. May 14, 2009. www.historynet.com/the-legendary-lockheed-constellation.htm

37. Flight of the Connie, Aviation History. "History: The Quest for Speed." www.flightoftheconnie.org/history

38. Sandvick, Gerald. "Enterprise in the Skies." *Minnesota History Magazine*, September 1, 1986. http://collections.mnhs.org/MNHistoryMagazine/articles/50/v50i03p086-098.pdf

39. Moylan, Martin. "Northwest Airlines: A Look Back at Its Long History." Minnesota Public Radio News. October 30, 2008. www.mprnews.org/story/2008/01/09/nwa_history

40. Moylan, Martin. "Northwest Airlines Mechanics Vote to End Strike." Minnesota Public Radio News. November 6, 2006. www.mprnews.org/story/2008/01/09/nwa_history

41. Romer, Christina D. "The Nation in Depression." *Journal of Economic Perspectives*, 1993, 19-39. Accessed September 24, 2014. http://elsa.berkeley.edu/~cromer/The Nation in Depression.pdf

42. U.S. Census Bureau. "Population of States and Counties of the United States: 1790 to 1990." U.S. Census Bureau. www.census.gov/population/www/censusdata/pop1790-1990.html

43. Tselos, George. "Self-help and Sauerkraut." *Minnesota History Magazine*, December 1, 1977. http://collections.mnhs.org/MNHistoryMagazine/articles/45/v45i08p306-320.pdf

44. The National Bureau of Economic Research. "The Welfare of Children During the Great Depression." April 1, 2002. www.nber.org/papers/w8902

45. Johnson, Frederick. "The Civilian Conservation Corps: A New Deal for Youth." *Minnesota History Magazine*, September 1, 1983. http://collections.mnhs.org/MNHistoryMagazine/articles/48/v48i07p295–302.pdf

46. United States. National Park Service. "The Civilian Conservation Corps." National Parks Service. September 16, 2014. www.nps.gov/voya/planyourvisit/ccc-general-history.htm

47. United States District Court, District of Minnesota. "History, Wilbur Foshay: An Empire Built on Paper." www.mnd.uscourts.gov/History/Foshay/Foshay01.pdf

48. *Ibid*.

49. Public Broadcasting System. "Lindbergh: Fallen Hero: Charles Lindbergh in the 1940s." www.pbs.org/wgbh/amex/lindbergh/sfeature/fallen.html

50. Bredemus, Jim. "The 'Lonely Eagle': Charles Lindbergh's Involvement in WWII Politics." Charles Lindbergh www.traces.org/charleslindbergh.html

51. Charles Lindbergh, An American Aviator. "Des Moines Speech: Delivered in Des Moines, Iowa, on September 11, 1941, This Speech Was Met with Outrage in Many Quarters." www.charleslindbergh.com/americanfirst/speech.asp

52. *Ibid*.

53. Weber, Laura. "Gentiles Preferred" Minneapolis Jews and Employment 1920–1950." *Minnesota History Magazine*, April 1, 1991. http://collections.mnhs.org/MNHistoryMagazine/articles/52/v52i05p166–182.pdf

54. *Ibid.*

55. Jewish Virtual Library. "Jews in America: Jewish Gangsters." https://www.jewishvirtuallibrary.org/jsource/US-Israel/gangsters.html

56. National Defense and the Canadian Forces. "12th Manitoba Dragoons." www.cmp-cpm.forces.gc.ca/dhh-dhp/his/ol-lo/vol-tom-3/par1/arm-bli/12MD-eng.asp

57. DePaulo, Lisa. "Who Killed the Gangster's Daughter?" NYMag.com. http://nymag.com/nymetro/news/crimelaw/features/4459/

58. Minnesota Historical Society. "World War II (1941-1945)." Historic Fort Snelling. www.historicfortsnelling.org/history/military-history/world-war-ii

59. Minnesota Historical Society, Minnesota's Greatest Generation. "Fort Snelling's Last War." www.mnhs.org/people/mngg/investigate/fswwii.php

60. Globalsecurity.org. "Twin Cities Army Ammunition Plant." www.globalsecurity.org/military/facility/aap-twincities.htm

61. Twin Cities Army Ammunition Plant Redevelopment. "TCAAP." http://tcaap.net

62. "St. Paul Ford Plant Timeline." *StarTribune*. www.startribune.com/components/134952973.html

63. Pugmire, Tim. "Last Few Minn. Pearl Harbor Vets Gather to Share Stories." Minnesota Public Radio News. December 7, 2011. www.mprnews.org/story/2011/12/07/last-few-minnesota-pearl-harbor-vets-gather-to-share-stories

64. Minnesota.gov. "Pearl Harbor Remembered." December 9, 2013. http://mn.gov/mdva/blog/blog-entry.jsp?id=367-100193

65. *Ibid.*

66. Minnesota Humanities Center. "Total Range Shipments of Iron Ore in Gross Tons." Minnesotahumanities.org. http://minnesotahumanities.org/Resources/Total Range Shipments.pdf

67. Worldsteel.org. "Steel and Raw Materials (Fact Sheet)." www.worldsteel.org/dms/internetDocumentList/fact-sheets/Fact-sheet_Raw-materials2011/document/Fact sheet_Raw materials2011.pdf

68. Bredemus, Jim. "The 'Lonely Eagle': Charles Lindbergh's Involvement in WWII Politics." Charles Lindbergh. www.traces.org/charleslindbergh.html

69. Smithsonian's National Air and Space Museum. "Charles Lindbergh." http://airandspace.si.edu/research/fellowships/lindbergh.cfm

70. *Ibid.*

71. TRACES.org. "The Legacy." www.traces.org/germanpows.html

72. Lobdell, George. "Minnesota's 1944 PW Escape." *Minnesota History Magazine,* September 1, 1964. http://collections.mnhs.org/MNHistoryMagazine/articles/54/v54i03p112-123.pdf

73. *Ibid.*

74. *Ibid.*

75. TRACES.org. "Internees: What Midwest Soldiers Found in Nazi Concentration Camps." www.traces.org/midwestliberators.html

76. Minnesota National Guard. "History of the 34th Infantry Division." www.minnesotanationalguard.org/units/34id/history.php

77. *Ibid.*

78. National Archives and Records Administration. "The Honor List of Missing and Dead for Minnesota." http://media.nara.gov/media/images/28/32/28-3153a.gif

79. National Archives and Records Administration. "World War II Honor List of Dead and Missing Army and Army Air Forces Personnel From: Minnesota." www.archives.gov/research/military/ww2/army-casualties/minnesota.html

80. Ano, Masaharu. "Nisei of World War II Learned Japanese in Minnesota." *Minnesota History Magazine*, September 1, 1977.

81. Nelson, Tim. "Vets Recall Deadly Korean War Battle." Minnesota Public Radio News. November 11, 2010. www.mprnews.org/story/2010/11/11/inver-grove-heights-veterans-day-ceremony

82. National Archives and Records Administration. "U.S. Military Fatal Casualties of the Korean War for Home-State-of-Record: Minnesota." www.archives.gov/research/military/korean-war/casualty-lists/mn-alpha.pdf

83. St. Louis Park Historical Society. "Civil Defense." www.slphistory.org/history/civildefense.asp

84. Radio Tapes. "WCCO Civil Defense Message 1961." www.radiotapes.com/WCCO/WCCO-AM_Civil_Defense_1961.mp3

85. Fitzgerald, John. "Minnesota Values Shaped Civil-rights Leader Roy Wilkins." *MinnPost*. January 18, 2013. www.minnpost.com/minnesota-history/2013/01/minnesota-values-shaped-civil-rights-leader-roy-wilkins

86. Risjord, Norman K. *A Popular History of Minnesota*. St. Paul, MN: Minnesota Historical Society Press, 2005.

87. *Ibid.*

88. Minnesota Historical Society. "Rondo Neighborhood & I-94." Gale Family Library, Research Guide, Rondo Neighborhood & I-94. Accessed September 25, 2014. http://libguides.mnhs.org/rondo

89. Public Art St. Paul. "Western Park Neighborhood History." www.publicartstpaul.org/downloads/westernhistory-1.pdf

90. Minnesota.gov. "Minnesota Vietnam Memorial." http://mn.gov/mdva/memorials/minnesotavietnammemorial.jsp

91. The Minneapolis Foundation. "Immigration in Minnesota, Discovering Common Ground." Minneapolisfoundation.org. www.minneapolisfoundation.org/uploads/cuteeditor/publications/community/immigrationbrochure.pdf

92. *Ibid*.

93. *Ibid*.

94. Love, Robertus. "Distribution of Immigrants: How Uncle Sam Intends to Properly Handle His Incoming Wards." *Princeton Union*, October 3, 1907. Library of Congress. Chronicling America Digital Newspaper Archive. http://chroniclingamerica.loc.gov/lccn/sn83016758/1907-10-03/ed-1/seq-2.pdf

SIDEBAR CITATIONS. NOTE, THEY ARE LISTED IN ORDER OF APPEARANCE. SIDEBARS ARE CITED WITH ROMAN NUMERALS INSTEAD OF NUMBERS.

DAKOTA AND OJIBWE INDIAN-INSPIRED PLACES AND NAMES

Dakota

I. City of Anoka, MN. "Anoka History." www.ci.anoka.mn.us/index.asp?Type=B_BASIC&SEC={C68813B5-53EA-4CE0-B0A0-968D82A2DA47}

II. City of Chanhassen. "History." www.ci.chanhassen.mn.us/index.aspx?NID=94

III. Willmar Lakes Area Convention and Visitors Bureau. "History of Kandiyohi County." www.willmarlakesarea.com/what-to-do/history

IV. Minneiska History Page. "The City of Minneiska." http://minneiska-mn.com/history/history.htm

V. Minnesota Department of Natural Resources. "Minneopa State Park." Minnesota DNR State Parks. www.dnr.state.mn.us/state_parks/minneopa/index.html

VI. Upham, Warren. *Minnesota Place Names: A Geographical Encyclopedia*. 3rd ed. St. Paul, Minn.: Minnesota Historical Society Press, 2001. Accessed via the Minnesota Historical Society online, http://mnplaces.mnhs.org/upham/

VII. Shakopee Mdewakanton Sioux Community. "Frequently Asked Questions about the Shakopee Mdewakanton Sioux Community." www.shakopeedakota.org/faq/index.php

VIII. Upham, Warren. *Minnesota Place Names: A Geographical Encyclopedia*. 3rd ed. St. Paul, Minn.: Minnesota Historical Society Press, 2001. Accessed via the Minnesota Historical Society online, http://mnplaces.mnhs.org/upham/

IX. *Ibid*.

X. Minnesota Historical Society. "Minnesota Is a Dakota Place." The U.S.-Dakota War of 1862. www.usdakotawar.org/history/dakota-homeland/minnesota-dakota-place

XI. Yellow Medicine County, Minnesota. "History of Yellow Medicine County, Minnesota." www.co.ym.mn.gov/index.asp?Type=B_BASIC&SEC={30AE3EFE-D26D-4C59-9900-BCC5DA82AC32}

Resources

Ojibwe

I. Upham, Warren. *Minnesota Place Names: A Geographical Encyclopedia*. 3rd ed. St. Paul, Minn.: Minnesota Historical Society Press, 2001. Accessed via the Minnesota Historical Society online, http://mnplaces.mnhs.org/upham/

II. Otter Tail County, Minnesota. "The Name "Otter Tail"" www.co.otter-tail.mn.us/573/The-Name-Otter-Tail

III. Upham, Warren. *Minnesota Place Names: A Geographical Encyclopedia*. 3rd ed. St. Paul, Minn.: Minnesota Historical Society Press, 2001. Accessed via the Minnesota Historical Society online, http://mnplaces.mnhs.org/upham/

IV. *Ibid.*

V. *Ibid.*

EUROPEAN PLACE NAMES IN MINNESOTA

I. Bois Forte Band of Chippewa. "Bois Forte - History." www.boisforte.com/history.htm

II. Upham, Warren. *Minnesota Place Names: A Geographical Encyclopedia*. 3rd ed. St. Paul, Minn.: Minnesota Historical Society Press, 2001. Accessed via the Minnesota Historical Society online, http://mnplaces.mnhs.org/upham

III. *Ibid.*

IV. Genealogical Society of Finland. "Finnish Place Names - Minnesota." www.genealogia.fi/place/placemne.htm

V. *Ibid.*

VI. Upham, Warren. *Minnesota Place Names: A Geographical Encyclopedia*. 3rd ed. St. Paul, Minn.: Minnesota Historical Society Press, 2001. Accessed via the Minnesota Historical Society online, http://mnplaces.mnhs.org/upham/

LUMBERJACK LINGO

I. Sorden, L.G., and Isabel Ebert. *Logger's Words of Yesterday*. Dubuque: WM. C. Brown, 1956. Accessed via the Murphy Library at the University of Wisconsin Lacrosse, http://murphylibrary.uwlax.edu/digital/wisc/loggers.pdf

II. *Ibid.*

III. *Ibid.*

IV. Online Etymology Dictionary. "Haywire" www.etymonline.com/index.php?term=haywire

V. "Minnesota Young Naturalists: Sweat Pads, Logging Berries and Blackjack." *Minnesota Conservation Volunteer*, Young Naturalists (online). November 1, 2008. V. http://files.dnr.state.mn.us/publications/volunteer/young_naturalists/logging/logging.pdf

VI. From Camp to Community: Loggers' Lingo. "Logging Lingo." www.camptocommunity.ca/english/lingo.html

VII. Sorden, L.G., and Isabel Ebert. *Logger's Words of Yesterday*. Dubuque: WM. C. Brown, 1956. Accessed via the Murphy Library at the University of Wisconsin Lacrosse, http://murphylibrary.uwlax.edu/digital/wisc/loggers.pdf

VIII. Larson, Agnes. "On the Trail of the Woodsman in Minnesota." *Minnesota History Magazine*, December 1, 1932, http://collections.mnhs.org/MNHistoryMagazine/articles/13/v13i04p349-366.pdf

FAMOUS TYCOONS AND LUMBER BARONS

I. Minnesota Encyclopedia, Minnesota Historical Society. "Lowry, Thomas (1843–1909)." www.mnopedia.org/person/lowry-thomas-1843

II. Minneapolis Institute of Arts. "Mission and History | Minneapolis Institute of Arts." http://new.artsmia.org/about/museum-info/mission-and-history/

TRIP TO THE GENERAL STORE: PRICES, THEN AND NOW

I. "F.J. Valek's Quit Business Sale." *Mower County Transcript*., December 30, 1914. Accessed via Chronicling America, Library of Congress, http://chroniclingamerica.loc.gov/lccn/sn85025431/1914-12-30/ed-1/seq-6.jp2

II. U.S. Bureau of Labor Statistics. "U.S. Bureau of Labor Statistics, Consumer Price Data." Accessed September 25, 2014. www.bls.gov/cpi/#tables

III. Price data obtained from Amazon.com and Walmart.com

BREWING IN MINNESOTA

I. Dunbar, Elizabeth, and Tim Nelson. "Schell's Brewery in New Ulm to Mark 150th Anniversary." Minnesota Public Radio News. December 21, 2009. www.mprnews.org/story/2009/12/21/schells-brewery-150

II. Webb, Tom. "Remembering: Theo. Hamm Brewing Co." TwinCities.com. October 10, 2009. www.twincities.com/business/ci_13473680

III. Urban Organics. "Urban Organics." http://urbanorganics.com

IV. City of Minneapolis, Community Planning and Economic Development. "Archaeological Investigation of the John Orth Brewing Company." www.minneapolismn.gov/www/groups/public/@cped/documents/webcontent/convert_279032.pdf

V. Fitger's Inn. "History." www.fitgers.com/subpage.php?page=History

A BRIEF CRIME TOUR OF MINNESOTA

I. Elder, Robert. "Execution 150 Years Ago Spurs Calls for Pardon." *New York Times*, December 13, 2010. www.nytimes.com/2010/12/14/us/14dakota.html?pagewanted=all&_r=1&

II. Bailey, James. "Citizens Confront James-Younger Gang: The Northfield Raid of 1876." Dr. Bailey's Applied Forensic Resources. https://mavdisk.mnsu.edu/bailej1/researchabstracts/research15.pdf

III. Visit Saint Paul. "Gangster Tour." www.visitsaintpaul.com/content/download/1658/19567/version/2/file/gangster

IV. Welter, Ben. "Wednesday, Dec. 5, 1928: St. Paul Gang Figure Slain." *Yesterdays News.* December 2, 2005. http://blogs2.startribune.com/blogs/oldnews/archives/52

V. Ode, Kim. "Swashbuckling in St. Paul: John Dillinger." *StarTribune*.com: News, Weather, Sports from Minneapolis, St. Paul and Minnesota. June 29, 2009. www.startribune.com/lifestyle/49452787.html

VI. City of Brainerd. "A Walk Through History, Downtown." www.ci.brainerd.mn.us/history/BrainerdHistoryWalk.pdf

VII. Collins, Bob. "The Day Baby Face Nelson Came to Brainerd." Minnesota Public Radio, NewsCut (blog). May 13, 2013. http://blogs.mprnews.org/newscut/2013/05/the_day_baby_face_nelson_came/

VIII. City of St. Paul. "St. Paul Police Department, Early History of the Police Department." www.stpaul.gov/Document Center/Home/View/1936

A BRIEF WALKING TOUR OF F. SCOTT FITZGERALD'S ST. PAUL

I. Kane, Patricia. "F. Scott Fitzgerald's St. Paul: A Writer's Use of Material." *Minnesota History Magazine*, December 1, 1976. http://collections.mnhs.org/MNHistoryMagazine/articles/45/v45i04p141-148.pdf

II. University of South Carolina Libraries. "A Fitzgerald Chronology." http://library.sc.edu/spcoll/fitzgerald/chronology.html

III. Caudle, Bill, and Barb Caudle. "F. Scott Fitzgerald Walking Tour of St. Paul, MN." Bill and Barb Caudle's Home Page. http://home.comcast.net/~caudle2/fscotwlk.htm

IV. Visit Saint Paul. Gangster Tour." www.visitsaintpaul.com/content/download/1658/19567/version/2/file/gangster

A MULTICULTURAL MENU

I. "Recipes from the Iron Range." Minnesota Public Radio News. May 21, 2006. www.mprnews.org/story/2006/05/16/rangerecipes

Photo Credits

All photos used in this book are being used legally. The book includes photos used pursuant to Creative Commons Licenses (see next page), public domain images, and other images that were obtained with permission from their photographers. As a courtesy, public domain resources/institutions were credited when possible. If you have questions about a photo source, please contact the author at www.brettortler.com.

Front cover
(from left to right): Library of Congress, Brett Ortler, Library of Congress, Brett Ortler, Library of Congress

The (unaltered) image on the far right is used in accordance with the Creative Commons 2.0 Attribution License, available here: http://creativecommons.org/licenses/by/2.0/

The image is "1st Minnesota at Gettysburg," by Don Troiani, Courtesy of the National Guard Flickr Page. Original available here: www.flickr.com/photos/thenationalguard/410109278

Back cover
Two (unaltered) back cover images are used in accordance with the Creative Commons 2.0 Attribution License, available here: http://creativecommons.org/licenses/by/2.0/

The topmost image is "Foshay Tower, Minneapolis, Minn./postcard," by Minneapolis College of Arts and Design Flickr Page. Original available here: www.flickr.com/photos/69184488@N06/10676825113/in/photolist-MCAD2.0

The second image from the bottom is "Mill City Museum from an Angle Minneapolis, MN" by Flickr User Richie Diesterheft. Original available here: www.flickr.com/photos/puroticorico/3611758075

The other back cover images are from stock resources or are in the public domain.

Interior photo credits

Page 10 Library of Congress **Page 11** Library of Congress **Page 20** Library of Congress **Page 21** Post Office of the Faroe Islands **Page 37** Library of Congress **Page 38** Brett Ortler **Page 39** Library of Congress **Page 40** Library of Congress **Page 41** (bottom) Library of Congress **Page 43** Library of Congress **Page 45** (top), Library of Congress **Page 48** Library of Congress **Page 51** Oldadsarefunny.blogspot.com **Page 54** (both) Library of Congress **Page 56** Brett Ortler **Page 58** Library of Congress **Page 59** New York Public Library **Page 60** Minneapolis Photo Collection, Central Library **Page 65** Library of Congress **Page 66** Library of Congress **Page 67** Library of Congress **Page 71** Adam Cuerden (original via Library of Congress) **Page 85** Brett Ortler **Page 86** Minneapolis Public Library **Page 87** U.S. National Archives **Page 91** Government Printing Office **Page 92** White House Press Office **Page 128** Kayli Schaaf

The following unaltered images are used in accordance with the Creative Commons 2.0 Attribution License, available here: http://creativecommons.org/licenses/by/2.0/

Page 13 "Homo sapiens neanderthalensis" by Wikipedia User Luna04. Original available here: http://commons.wikimedia.org/wiki/File:Homo_sapiens_neanderthalensis.jpg

Page 32 "3678 Mississippi Headwaters Itasca State Park Minnesota," by Flickr User Bill McChesney, Original available here: www.flickr.com/photos/bsabarnowl/5361564073

Page 49 "1st Minnesota at Gettysburg," by Don Troiani, Courtesy of the National Guard Flickr Page. Original available here: www.flickr.com/photos/thenationalguard/4101092782

Page 83 "Foshay Tower, Minneapolis, Minn./postcard," by Minneapolis College of Arts and Design Flickr Page. Original available here: www.flickr.com/photos/69184488@N06/10676825113/in/photolist-MCAD2.0

The following unaltered image is used in accordance with the Creative Commons 3.0 Attribution License, available here: http://creativecommons.org/licenses/by/3.0/deed.en

Page 22 "Beaver Hat," by Wikipedia User Themightyquill. Original available here: http://commons.wikimedia.org/wiki/File:Beaver-felt-hat-ftl.jpg

Recommended Reading

RECOMMENDED READING

Blegen, Theodore. *Minnesota: A History of the State*. Minneapolis, MN: University Of Minnesota Press, 1975.

Gibbon, Guy. *Archaeology of Minnesota: The Prehistory of the Upper Mississippi River Region*. Minneapolis, MN: University of Minnesota Press, 2012.

Pennefeather, Shannon M. *Mill City: A Visual History of the Minneapolis Mill District*. St. Paul, MN: Minnesota Historical Society Press, 2003.

Westerman, Gwen, and Bruce White. *Mni Sota Makoce: The Land of the Dakota*. St. Paul, MN: Minnesota Historical Society Press.

Risjord, Norman K. *A Popular History of Minnesota*. St. Paul, MN: Minnesota Historical Society Press, 2005.

Upham, Warren. *Minnesota Place Names: A Geographical Encyclopedia*. 3rd ed. St. Paul, MN.: Minnesota Historical Society Press, 2001.

ONLINE RESOURCES

Minnesota Historical Society
www.mnhs.org

Minnesota Department of Natural Resources
www.dnr.state.mn.us/

MNopedia: Minnesota Encyclopedia
www.mnopedia.org/

Minnesota History Magazine
www.mnhs.org/market/mhspress/minnesotahistory/

The U.S.-Dakota War of 1862
www.usdakotawar.org

About the Author

Brett Ortler is the author of *The Fireflies Book*, *The Mosquito Book* and *Minnesota Trivia: Don'tcha Know!*. An editor at Adventure Publications, he has edited dozens of books, including many field guides and nature-themed books. His work appears widely, including in *Salon*, *The Good Men Project*, *The Nervous Breakdown*, *Living Ready* and in a number of other venues in print and online. He lives in the Twin Cities with his wife and their young son. For more, visit www.brettortler.com.